SECONDS TO DISASTER

US EDITION

By Glenn Meade

And

Ray Ronan

SECONDS TO DISASTER

By Glenn Meade

And

Ray Ronan

****

Published by:

Glenn Meade And Ray Ronan

Copyright (c) 2012 by Glenn Meade And Ray Ronan

Cover By Ho Creative Design

****

Licence Notes

ISBN-13:

978-1481026437

ISBN-10:

1481026437

****

Foreword

by

Tim van Beveren

pilot, aviation editor &

safety analyst.

I've loved to fly since my early childhood and flew a lot with my parents since I was three years old. I saw the change from propeller driven aircraft to the jet age, the introduction of the Boeing 747 Jumbo Jet, the supersonic Concorde and the newly fly-by-wire technology of modern Airbus family aircraft and all of that "hooked" me.

At the age of sixteen, I started to fly myself. Small aircraft first, then I got my license to operate engine powered aircraft. Eventually, I learned to fly a jet and got myself the training to operate a Boeing 737. But I had no desire to become an airline pilot. I flew for fun and not to make a living. For my job as a journalist, I have to fly a lot to the remotest of places and I still enjoy it every time, especially during the moment of acceleration on the runway until the aircraft wheels gently leave the ground and we are up in the air.

If you would like to maintain this enthusiastic and positive picture of aviation for yourself, you better put this book down right now.

But if you want to inform yourself about what is currently wrong in the aviation field and why, you should carefully continue reading.

I personally never encountered any fear of flying, not as a passenger or as a pilot, especially when I was operating an aircraft that I was familiar with and where I could depend on the engineers to properly perform their job in keeping it 100 percent airworthy.

This is because my thinking and my actions are subject to a fundamental principle since my first flight lesson: the precautionary principle.

In aviation, it is especially vital to look ahead. "Never fly your aircraft anywhere where you haven't already travelled in your mind. "This is one of the basic principles commonly repeated by flight instructors and it is still valid, despite the advanced technological achievements in aviation that we encountered during the now more than 100 years in which humans have learned to master the skies. What made flying safe in the past 100 years was sticking to the precautionary principle and to "live" it.

Accidents and incidents have to be avoided. But if they do happen, they have to be thoroughly analysed and the findings have to be shared, so they may not repeat themselves. This also implies "sharing your experience" in a non-punitive environment, meaning you may freely admit a mistake or an error that you made, so others can learn from it.

The principle of flying hasn't changed since the famous Wright brothers took off in Kitty Hawk in 1903. What has changed is that today we are facing innovations at a very fast pace. Modern aircraft with advanced systems, new materials, range and comfort aboard on the one hand, and national and international regulations and standards on the other. The latter is intended to ensure that flying is subject to the highest and safest standards that one could think of. A very good intention, but unfortunately it has long been compromised by cost and profit-driven decisions by airline management, and political lobbying by vested interests within the transportation sector.

For millions of travellers the most important issue whenever they board an aircraft is safety. Of course, there will never be a level that will insure 100 percent safety. Therefore, we will probably never see a time of zero incidents or accidents. But many disasters could have been prevented—if only the causes had been properly analysed by the relevant supervising agencies, and if aviation managers responsible had been willing to learn from the mistakes that led to a disaster.

Air travel is safe - so they say. But incidents and accidents occur even in a supposed "safe environment", and these are always a concern for the experts who analyse such events in order to prevent future tragedies.

However, it seems that the rules today when it comes to improving air safety have more to do with economic considerations on behalf of airline management and their overseeing government authorities. This contradictory liaison has often played a sinister role in recent air disasters, examples of which you will find in this book.

Another vital problem is this: passengers don't have the same powerful lobbies as the aviation industry. Their safety should be protected by parliamentarians. But few politicians have a true understanding of this very specialized field, or are qualified enough to know exactly what needs to done to improve safety for the traveling public.

Sadly, it is a mistake to believe that in aviation the highest standards still apply. Safety costs money and at times of low-cost traveling the airlines are left with narrowing margins, which can mean less money to invest in maintaining a safe operation. Often,

Seconds To Disaster

the daily burden of ensuring a safe flight is shouldered more and more by the weakest part in the safety chain: the pilots.

The "human factor" is currently the main factor when aviation accidents occur. But this is not limited to mistakes made by pilots. It also applies to maintenance, airline management, aircraft and component manufacturers and national and international supervising authorities, who are responsible for the "safety net" that should surround each and every flight. But if the net is torn, it is just a matter of time before the hole become big enough for an Airbus A380 with 800 passengers, or its counterpart—a newly Boeing 747-800—falls through the net, and with massively fatal consequences.

You will learn in the chapters such as the ones about the ill-fated flight of Air France 447 about deficiencies well known and identified long before the fatal accident.

You will also learn about design deficiencies in the system layout of the most advanced and highly computerized aircraft of the world—and the problems of the so called "man-machine interface" which makes it difficult for the human being in charge to operate this complex system, especially when the automation fails. Shortcuts in the requirements for training are also believed to have played a key role in the AF447 disaster.

You will read about airlines you should consider twice about flying with, for the cheap fares they offer may well risk the lives of you and your loved ones if you happen to be their passengers. On the subject of your loved ones: you will learn about the lethal effect of the nice little baby-belt your flight attendant will hand you for your toddler on board, if your child is under the age of two years. This device is not intended to protect your kid in the case of a disaster striking, but will most likely severely injure or even kill it.

Or have you ever wondered why you felt so dizzy and had a headache after you noticed a strange smell aboard your aircraft? Did it ever cross your mind that you were just poisoned with a nerve agent? Read about one of the best kept secrets of the industry for decades.

This book offers some frightening examples of highly dangerous airline practices that affect the travelling public, and also sounds a warning bell. The European Aviation Safety Agency (EASA) is responsible for setting European standards that apply to all EU member states, their airlines, training facilities, their manufactures of aircraft and their components. It gets its power from the public. Yet recent activities of this agency, such as their reaction to toxic cabin air, child safety or pilot fatigue, demonstrate that the authority rather tends to follow the economically driven considerations of those whom the agency is supposed to regulate: the European airlines and the powerful international aviation industry.

The ambition of these airlines and its industry is to survive in an incredibly fast growing market that is driven by globalization rather than the desire to maintain the highest level of safety that protects both passengers and air crews.

The USA is facing a similar problem—all decisions for safety improvements have to go through a crucial cost – benefit analysis first. In a TV interview I once conducted with the US democratic Congressman Peter deFazio, a well-known critical member of the Transportation Committee of Congress, he didn't mince words: "If it is cheaper to kill people, then we kill people!" It seems Europe and the EASA is also diverting down this unethical, immoral and highly dangerous path.

Hopefully the EASA and the FAA—the key major players when it comes to regulation and safety in aviation—will get back on track before it's too late and more disasters have struck. A proverb among safety experts is: "If you want to know the costs of safety, try an accident." Of course, this should never be an option.

I'm convinced that this book and its publication will well remind them of this duty.

Tim van Beveren
Berlin, May 15th 2012

Acknowledgements:

Flight Safety Foundation

Michael J. Dreikorn, Ed.D. | Federal Aviation Administration Inspector | ASD experts

Professor Ed Galea | Fire Engineering Safety Group, University of Greenwich.

Captain John Hoyte | Chairman Aerotoxic Association.

Teamsters | Airline Division, United States.

Gerry Byrne | Aviation Investigative Journalist. Flight 427 Anatomy of an Air Disaster.

Dr. Michael Dreikorn | The IPL Group

Professor Ed Galea and the Fire Engineering Safety Group team | University of Greenwich.

John Greaves | Aviation Attorney and former Airline Captain Baum Hedlund Law

Captain John Hoyte | Chairman Aerotoxic Association.

Teamsters | Airline Division, United States.

SNPL | Syndicat National des Pilotes de Ligne (National Union of Airline Pilots; France)

ECA | European Cockpit Association

Tim Van Beveren | pilot, aviation editor & safety analyst

German Pilots Association

Jan Brown | Former flight attendant now campaigner for children's safety onboard.

Pilots and other aviation employees who cannot be named. Thank you all for your support and trust. We hope this book helps us generate debate and help turn back the tide from 'profit, and then passengers', to, 'passengers, and then profit.'

Chapter 1

LOST

Air France Flight 447

It was no night for dying.

In Rio De Janeiro that late May the temperature hung close to eighteen degrees. It was approaching midwinter in Brazil but that night the air was balmy, not a breath of wind whispered in the humid air. On Copacabana Beach, the sea glassy calm, promenades thronged with families and lovers enjoying a stroll, groups of tanned teenage boys and girls lazing in the sand, laughing and playing music.

On the Avenue Del Flores, the Volkswagen bus carrying the twelve Air France crew led by Captain Marc Dubois set out from the Hilton Hotel at seven-thirty p.m. The crew bus stop-started in the heavy rush-hour traffic. As usual, pick-up was two and a half hours before the flight's scheduled take-off to allow ample room for road delays. The bus driver on duty that evening always tried to be on time and waited duly outside the hotel entrance for his crew.

'It was such a pleasant night,' Oscar Hernandez, a member of the hotel staff remembered. 'The crew was in good spirits. They could certainly have had no intuition that a terrible disaster was about to unfold. That they were being driven to their unspeakable deaths.'

1

Among the crew bus passengers, thirty-two year old Air France co-pilot Pierre-Cedric Bonin had started flying the Airbus A330 in April. His young wife Isabelle had come along with him on the trip and she talked about how much she had loved her brief two-day stopover in Rio.

The second co-pilot, David Robert—on extended long-haul international flights, the practice is to have a third cockpit crewmember—had 6,600 flight hours with Air France and had qualified to fly the A330 in 2002.

Their captain, Marc Dubois, at fifty, was a veteran pilot. Since June 1998 he had accumulated over 1700 hours on the A330 alone and flew the four engine A340, a common practice in airlines, which had both types on their fleet. This was his seventeenth rotation in the South America sector.

But unknown to Captain Marc Dubois and his fellow crew as they chatted on the short thirty-minute trip to the airport, Air France Flight 447, bound for Paris over 5000 miles away on a long journey over the dark, turbulent waters of the Atlantic, that night was to be their last.

*

At Antonio Carlos Jobim International Airport, the crew climbed down from the bus for what they assumed would be just another leg home. The overcast sky held the temperature and humidity constant. Captain Dubois talked with his crew as they waited for their bags, co-pilot Bonin hurried off with his wife to help her check in.

The bus driver offloaded the last of the luggage and Captain

Dubois' crew wheeled their suitcases inside. Purser Anne Grimout, a forty-nine year-old from Ermenonville, in Normandy, had worked for Air France for nearly twenty-five years. She chatted with Lucas Gagliano, who was the only Brazilian national working on the flight. Twenty-three year-old Lucas had returned to Brazil to attend his father's funeral two weeks before.

After queuing up for passport control, Captain Dubois left the flight attendants to their own preparations, while he led his two first officers to Air France operations.

In the office, Dubois was handed the briefing pack for AF447 by the flight departure agent and sat down with Robert and Bonin to plan their flight from Rio to Paris. Meanwhile, an arriving Air France A330-200, registered as F-GZCP, touched down on the main runway and taxied to its stand.

Ground staff at once commenced preparation of the jet for its next flight. The two Air France crew's paths never crossed. The incoming crew had reported no major snags or malfunctions. Once refueled, the aircraft was good to go, part of a continuous cycle of usage that is the lot of modern aircraft. Down time is money lost. The more time an aircraft is in use, the more profit the company makes.

In the briefing room, Dubois and his first officers studied their route. Weather in the mid-Atlantic at that time of year could be intense, massive storms a real threat. With no air traffic control facilities mid-Atlantic, a pilot must rely on preflight planning, reports from other aircraft enroute and their own aircraft's radar to negotiate a way around such storms. Severe weather systems were forecast.

But Dubois had often flown this route before and all in all, it looked as if it was going to be another routine flight.

While Dubois and his crew finished going over the flight plan, their passengers were already proceeding through check-in and immigration procedures. Two hundred and sixteen passengers consisted of thirty-two nationalities. They included a baby and seven other children. Sixty-one passengers were French citizens; fifty-eight were Brazilian and twenty-eight German.

Thirty-four year-old Swede Christine Schnabl and her five-year-old son Philippe were checked in and waiting for the flight. Christine, living in Brazil for 10 years, worked for the Swedish Chamber of Commerce in Rio and missed her relations in Sweden.

Her husband Fernando and their three-year-old daughter Celine had flown to Paris earlier with a different airline, intending to travel together for the homeward journey to Sweden for a holiday. According to one newspaper report, the Rio-based family always flew separately. Mr. and Mrs. Schnabl always feared they would all die together if their airplane crashed, and so they booked different flights.[1]

It was a decision that was going to tear this loving family apart forever.

By the time everyone was onboard it was already past scheduled departure of p.m. local, 22 h 00 UTC. The flight attendant's headcount confirmed the numbers. Captain Dubois signed the load sheet and the ground crew said 'bon voyage' before closing the door.

Ground crew confirmed pre-departure checks were complete and just before 22 h 10, the flight crew called the tower for pushback and engine start and they received the clearance to do so.

Satisfied that everything was as it should be, Captain Dubois called for brake release. At 22 h 10, Flight 447 pushed back from the gate. A short taxi later, the A330 powered down the runway, increasing speed until it climbed gracefully into the air at 22 h 29 mins.

Once airborne the crew contacted Rio De Janeiro approach control and soon after were passed over to the Curitiba air traffic control center which cleared them to climb to thirty-five thousand feet—FL 350—at 22 h 45.

Like many modern airlines Air France equip their aircraft with aviation's equivalent to a fax or SMS facility called ACARS[2].

At 22 h 51, via ACARS, the crew asked for and received the weather pertaining to the Brazilian airfields of Belo Horizonte, Salvador de Bahia and Recife.

These were airfields Captain Dubois was keeping in mind should he have need of a bolt hole in the highly unlikely event of an emergency.

But that night, the unlikely was about to happen.

*

Almost six thousand miles away in Paris, France, and nearly three hours later—02.10 UTC—a chatter of mysterious automated computer error messages were transmitted from the fight deck of Dubois' Airbus to the Air France operations office at Charles De Gaulle Airport.

Personnel on duty that night were horrified by a long list of ACARS signals that suddenly exploded on their screens.

One remembered staring open-mouthed at the arriving messages. 'It was so unreal. All of us who saw the ACARS communications coming from Fight 447 knew that something truly awful, something catastrophic was happening before our eyes.'

The cascade of messages signaled a calamitous series of events was unfolding on board the Airbus A330 above the turbulent Atlantic.

Operations staff watched their screens in utter disbelief. 'The failure messages kept coming,' another staff member on duty recalled. 'But there were no Mayday signals, no radio voice signals transmitted from the cockpit. There was no evidence of any emergency transmissions directly from the crew.'

In the space of only four minutes, twenty-four encoded messages were transmitted, signaling unreliable sensor data, autopilot disconnect and a series of colossal sub-systems failures on board the Airbus.

At 02.14 the last message was transmitted from Dubois' flight deck, indicating either a massive decompression failure or that the aircraft was moving with extremely high vertical velocity, or both, for the cabin was dropping at faster than thirty feet a second—an incredible rate.

In Paris, personnel on duty in the operations' office that morning anxiously watched their computers but no further signals were received from the stricken airliner that only moments before was powering its way through the stormy darkness above the Atlantic.

Air France Flight 447, with two hundred and twenty-eight passengers and crew on board, had disappeared from their screens without a trace.

Chapter 2

In Search of Answers

Why Air Accidents Happen

'The flying schedule comes first.' A UK airline CEO statement at a management meeting, Oct 2010.

There is a saying of Einstein's that is much quoted in the field of air crash investigation, or indeed any field that demands critical analytical skills—look long enough at a problem and an answer will present itself.

The fall of Air France Flight 447 was an unusual event. Unusual because it was marked by no emergency calls from the cockpit crew, no mayday signals, no last minute communications that could have hinted at why the aircraft simply vanished.

And unusual because catastrophic air accidents rarely happen in mid-flight. Most accidents occur within a critical eleven minute window of the flight phase, during take-off and landing.

Aircraft don't typically fall out of the sky.

And long before such a catastrophe might happen, a series of significant events has usually been set in motion, which may later offer causal clues to accident investigators.

In the case of Air France 447, though few solid answers were at first evident, the vast and deep Atlantic was soon about to offer up the first indications of what may have occurred.

*

Three days after Flight 447 disappeared the first physical evidence began to materialize. Eventually, fifty-three bodies of crew and passengers, an almost complete tail section, and numerous aircraft parts had been found floating near the accident zone, within the first week. They indicated, as investigators had suspected, that Flight 447 had suffered a catastrophic disaster.

An oceanographic research vessel, The Pourquoi Pas?, which was busily mapping the Mid-Atlantic Ridge where three tectonic plates confront each other at depths of up to five miles, had been called in to aid the underwater search. Part-owned by the French navy, the vessel carried onboard two mini-submarines. One of the subs, the Nautilus, had brought much of the great Titanic's treasures to the surface. The Nautilus was one of the few submarines in the world capable of descending to and trawling the deep oceans where Captain Dubois' Airbus had disappeared.

However, after four weeks of scouring the ocean depths for evidence of the crash, the sub failed to locate the aircraft remains, or the black box.

'The black boxes may never be found,' said Paul-Louis Arslanian, the head of the French enquiry. 'And it may not matter. We've had cases where we never found the black boxes and we were able to reconstruct what happened, and there have been cases where we found them and they didn't tell us anything useful.'

Glenn Meade/Ray Ronan

Yet unless you have all the evidence in front of you, nothing can be discounted. For without answers, without connecting the dots to give a true picture of all the factors that contributed to the disappearance of Flight 447, another airliner could suffer the same fate.

Although the aircraft—registered as F-GZCP—had completed 2644 take offs and landings the catastrophic problem or problems which surfaced that disastrous evening, on that particular flight, could go back a long way. Of course, eventually the black boxes were found and the evidence soon pointed to a catastrophic accident that, sadly, was avoidable.

Certainly some of the evidence will be a shock to readers, unfamiliar with cockpit crew procedure and airline industry policies.

Much of the time air crashes, as we will see, are a confluence of events—a cascade of bad luck, bad decisions, inappropriate airline company policy, insufficient training and failure of regulatory authority or various combinations of all five as well as other factors.

Some of that bad luck is often aided by the airline industry itself. We believe that some of its guiding principles—an endless and aggressive pursuit of bottom-line profit—no doubt contribute to the creeping erosion of safety standards, which puts both passenger and crew lives at serious risk.

There are more incidents, a term used for near accidents or events which could have led to an accident, than you may imagine and it's the increase in these incidents which is causing concern.

Many major accidents are often preceded by similar incidents in which it was only by coincidence that a loss did not occur.

Air crash investigators tell us that for every accident there were hundreds of similar incidences; if so, are fatal accidents the only gauge of airline safety?

NASA's Aviation Safety Reporting System, ASRS, collects confidential reports sent to it by airline industry workers. Their system indicates a marked increase in the number of incidences reported in recent years—and NASA says the true number of reports could be far greater.

It is possible that many who work in the US airline industry either do not know about the system or fear using it. But according to NASA, 'More than 975,000 reports have been submitted to date and no reporter's identity has ever been breached. We de-identify reports before entering them into the incident database.'[1]

The team at NASA believes such a system is vital: 'When organizations want to learn more about the occurrence of events, the best approach is simply to ask those involved.'[2]

With the growth of aircraft size and passenger capacity, when accidents occur they could well be monumental disasters. It is true that 2010 was the safest year with regards to loss of aircraft. But in 2011 the safety improvement was *modest* at best. [3] The number of people killed did not trend down but upwards. The number of incidents reported did not trend down but upwards.

It is common knowledge among flight safety experts that the last decade can be regarded as 'the lost decade', because of the lack of improvements in flight safety matters made in that period.

This book will not only pose and answer questions as to *why* accidents happen, but also offer solutions as to how they can be further prevented. It will also make passengers aware of how *they* can consciously limit their risk.

Glenn Meade/Ray Ronan

Simple but smart choices by passengers can make a huge difference in reducing their risk of exposure to danger while they and their families are flying.

In a world where air travel is set to grow at an exponential rate in the coming decades, this book will teach you how to fly smart and safe as a passenger.

It will teach you how to avoid the potential pitfalls that exist in commercial aviation—pitfalls that can sometimes expose unknowing air travelers to increased risk of being involved in a fatal air accident. In conversations and meetings with other pilots and industry experts, we learned about what *they* do to make their flight safer for crew and passengers.

This information should be shared with the public.

There is an even more contentious issue we intend to explore: what parts do both the airline industry and the worldwide aviation authorities responsible for governing that industry contribute in playing dice with passenger lives? And play dice they certainly do, through negligence and collusion, as the following pages will reveal.

The reality is many insiders in the airline business will concede that Air France Flight 447 was an accident that never should have happened, but was waiting to happen.

And the real tragedy, like so many of the disastrous accidents and terrifying incidents you are about to read about, is that scores of such calamities could well have been avoided by the airline industry and its watchdog authorities.

It's a theme that we will be returning to in the chapters ahead—how each and all of our lives are put at increasing risk daily when we fly and for one reason only.

The aggressive pursuit of profit—and the erosion of safety standards caused by that same relentless pursuit.

A pursuit, as we will see especially affects the lives and careers of airline cockpit crew, for it is in their professional hands that we place ourselves each time we fly.

And when crews go wrong, *everything* goes wrong.

Chapter 3

The Pilot's State of Mind

When Things Go Wrong in the Cockpit

Fans of the actor Robin Williams may recall one of his stand-up sketches. Acting the part of an airline captain, he steps on stage to give his pre-flight public announcement and in the process confesses his own troubles. 'Good morning, ladies and gentlemen, this is your captain speaking and welcome on board your flight,' Williams' spiel begins.

'Not terrific weather out there, I think you'll agree. It's raining pretty hard, with some bad gusting and there's some amazing lightning over on the port side if you're interested. Wow! See that flash? Not a great morning for flying, is it? Hey, I guess it's not exactly a great morning for me either. To tell the truth, my wife left me last night. After twenty years of marriage.'

She said that she couldn't live with my depressive moods anymore and that I was dragging her down. I ask you, after twenty years?

Have you any idea of the kind of mental anguish that can cause a man? I mean, I've been sitting up all night just thinking about those cruel words and they've cut the damned heart out of me.'

Williams pauses, wipes imaginary tears from his eyes, then beams a manic smile.

'But hey, that's enough about me, who wants to hear about my problems? So how about we just speed this big metal bird down the runway and up into the sky and see what the hell happens?'

*

At that stage, wise passengers would be running, screaming for the exits.

The point is pilots are human. They cut and bleed just like everyone else.

The vast majority are very professional men and women. Some have displayed inordinate courage, heroism, skill, tenacity and ability, protecting their passengers' lives in catastrophic aviation incidents.

They are not supermen, or women, but ordinary people just like you and me. You see them in the supermarket, pushing trolleys. You meet them in the golf club, or in a restaurant or bar.

You may know them as neighbors, relatives, brothers or sisters, casual acquaintances or friends. Like everyone else, they have their weaknesses and strengths, their vices and virtues. Like everyone else, they often have to bear their share of life's problems.

Among their number are counted all religions, and atheists and agnostics. They can be family-oriented men and women, or singles, philanderers, homosexuals, lesbians or transvestites. You name it, the cockpit's seen them all—neither should anyone care what their crews' orientation is so long as it doesn't interfere with the carrying out of their job nor in any way affect their level of professional skills.

Some pilots live quiet, purposeful lives. Others have stormy relationships or affairs, and battle with inner demons. As evidence, some have been removed from or arrested on aircraft while under the influence of alcohol—aircraft they were about to board and fly, laden with hundreds of passengers whose care had been placed in their hands. And as we shall see in the next chapter, some—like Williams' fictional captain—have troubled personal lives, which can sometimes cause them to experience nervous breakdowns mid-flight, and with dire and even deadly consequences.

Sometimes, like everyone else, pilots get overtired or don't feel too good on a day when they have to do their job. And what an important job it is—the fate of dozens or perhaps hundreds of lives might rest daily in their hands. Yet with the rise of low-fares carriers that pare costs to the bone, it is a job that it is increasingly poorly paid when one considers the expertise, training requirements and responsibilities demanded of pilots.

The industry in recent years has experienced what insiders call 'a dumbing down.' Salaries have been cut, training budgets have been trimmed. Command-hour requirements—the standards needed to attain the pilot rank of captain—have at times been drastically reduced because airlines want their new captains younger, cheaper and inherently less experienced.

It may surprise readers to learn in this book that there are pilots flying in the US whose salaries are so low they qualify for food stamps; they live in crash pads, time-sharing bunks with other crews because they cannot afford a place of their own.

This problem is not unique to the US.

In the United Kingdom there are pilots who live in squalid trailers within earshot of London's bustling Heathrow International Airport, because LIKE their US counterparts, they cannot afford to pay for transport costs and decent accommodation out of dismal salaries. It's also not unknown for junior co-pilots of prime low fares carriers to sleep overnight in cars between duties.

We will explore such issues later, for dozens of air carriers worldwide pay their pilots comparatively meager salaries and some none at all—men and women whose skill sets and well-being govern the fate of hundreds of thousands of people who travel on passenger aircraft on thousands of commercial flights on five continents daily around the world.

Lives, it seems, are sometimes almost as cheap as the low-fare tickets that many passengers seek.

*

Not surprisingly in this modern world the pilot's share of emotional and psychological problems are on the rise, as shown in a report commissioned by the British Airline Pilots Association. It found levels of self-reported fatigue, sleep problems and symptoms of anxiety and depression higher than would be expected in a general population.[1]

Aviation is not restricted by borders; is it safe to assume these problems are not exclusive to Europe and may be an issue in the US and elsewhere?

And this type of study does not appear to have been carried out in the US, yet since Jet Blue Capt. Clayton Osbon had a breakdown mid-flight in March of 2012, there have been calls

Glenn Meade/Ray Ronan

for stricter mental screening of pilots, to prevent mentally unstable crew from entering cockpits.[2] Judging by the frightening results of the British survey there appears to be dangerous situation brewing. Perhaps it's the increasing pressures placed on those crew that needs to be investigated?

Although much of it is due to life's increasingly demanding stresses that affect us all, including financial pressures, in the case of pilots it means heavier work schedules, extra flying hours, and as a result, increased fatigue. And as any pilot will tell you, fatigue in the cockpit is a deadly beast.

Mental and physical fatigue, along with overwork and long duty hours, have led to confusion and errors in the cockpit; which in turn have led to potentially serious incidents and to fatal accidents causing many thousands of deaths and injuries in air crashes over the years. In fact fatigue is known to be a factor in 20 percent of aircraft accidents.

Lesser known by the public, suicide has also been committed in the cockpit by stressed and mentally unstable pilots, and with deadly results.

The US government estimates that about 31,000 Americans die each year as a result of suicide. Worldwide, the number is in the millions. There are many motives—depression, shame, rage, anger, loss of love. But when problems overflow into pilots' professional lives and they kill themselves in the course of their duty hours, during a flight, there is often the added massive tragedy of the deaths of passengers.

Fortunately, the majority of pilots are highly-competent, highly-trained, professional men and women whose skills help prevent accidents, not cause them. But because humans are sometimes unpredictable, and because there is no such thing as absolute security, that protection can never be entirely guaranteed. There are rogue pilots who don't pay attention to the rules, pilots who falsify log books pretending to have more flight experience than they actually do, pilots who claim they were captains with their previous companies who in fact were always first officers, all to get a job. There are pilots who perhaps should never be allowed fly an airplane with fare paying passengers onboard.

John Greaves is an ex-airline captain with over 10,000 hours of flight time. A seasoned airline accident lawyer, Greaves has witnessed the heartache of families and loved ones of hundreds of airline accident victims in more than 35 airline disasters, including 911 victims. 'Airlines are upgrading captains, who have no business being captains,' he says and he is not alone in his thoughts. Thankfully, the rogues are an extreme minority.

However, as the events of September 11th vividly demonstrated though, sometimes the mad, the bad and the truly dangerous can slip through the net.

Chapter 4

Flight Decks, Drugs, and Audio Tape

Pilots with a Death Wish

For most of his life, to everyone who knew him, Japan Airlines Captain Seiji Katagiri seemed like a really nice guy.

A professional pilot who occasionally enjoyed playing golf in his spare time, he had flown for Japan Airlines for much of his twenty-two year career. The father of two children, he and his wife lived in Tokyo's middle-class suburb of Yeisha, in a neat two-story house a short drive from the city' airport of Haneda.

But Katagiri had a troubled mind.

When he began suffering from hallucinations and depression, his wife worried about his behavior. Katagiri once summoned police to his home and tried to convince them his home was bugged. A police search turned up no listening devices.

On at least three occasions his boss urged him to seek psychiatric help. Katagiri was given a month's leave.

When he returned to the flight deck, on February 9th, 1982, he captained Flight 350, a domestic crossing from Fukuoka to Tokyo. However, his employer, JAL, had not ensured that a vital company requirement be complied with—before Katagiri's reinstatement as a captain he would have to log at least twenty-five hours of supervised flying time.

It was a mistake that contributed to the chilling event that next unfolded.

As Katagiri made the final approach into Tokyo, the captain cracked-up at the controls and threw two of the DC-8's engines into reverse, which caused the plane to plunge into the icy waters of Tokyo Bay, three hundred yards short of the runway.

Twenty-four people died needlessly that day.

Katagiri survived and was one of the first to be taken aboard the rescue boat—unthinkable for a captain to be among the first to leave his ship—muttering to himself and telling his rescuers that he was an office worker. Katagiri later told police he felt ill on the morning of the flight. 'Then just before landing, I felt nausea, a feeling of terror and lost consciousness.'

Captain Katagiri was eventually found to be mentally ill. Tried, he was found not guilty by reason of insanity and detained in a secure psychiatric unit.[1]

Captain Katagiri isn't the only pilot who has snapped on the flight deck and decided to kill himself and his passengers, and no doubt he won't be the last.

In August 1994, on a domestic Royal Air Maroc flight to Casablanca from Agadir, the young captain, Younes Khyati, thirty-two, decided not just to end his own life, but those of his forty-eight passengers. An experienced pilot with 4,500 flying hours, Khyati was physically fit and had undergone a rigorous annual medical examination a month previous.

He showed no outward signs of mental illness, or psychological troubles.

But ten minutes after take-off, Khyati inexplicably switched off the autopilot at 15,000 feet and nosed the aircraft straight down. The female co-pilot radioed Casablanca. 'Mayday, Mayday, the pilot is—.' The message ended abruptly as the pilot plunged the airliner into the Atlas Mountains, killing everyone on board.

Motives have never been found to explain what crash investigators called Captain Khyati's 'incomprehensible gesture.'

Some suicide-by-pilot cases are even more bizarre. And none more bizarre than Egypt Air Flight 990.

The exact reason for the crash is still disputed by US and Egyptian authorities, who offered conflicting factors. Both US and Egyptian authorities conducted a joint investigation. Yet all the available facts point to an undeniable, chilling scenario that unfolded on board the scheduled Los Angeles-New York-Cairo flight on October 31, 1999.

At approximately 01.50 EST. Egypt Air Flight 990—a Boeing 767 named Tuthmosis III after a pharaoh from the 8th Dynasty— plunged into the Atlantic, sixty miles south of Nantucket Island, Massachusetts, in International waters. All 217 passengers on board were killed.

A rigorous investigation by US investigators concluded that the aircraft was crashed deliberately, in a case of pilot-suicide. One of the flight crew, First Officer Gameel Al-Batouti took charge of the flight controls when the captain excused himself to go to the bathroom, a conversation which was recorded by the cockpit voice recorder.

Thirty seconds later the voice recorder registered First Officer Al-Batouti, who was then alone in the cockpit, say, "I rely on God."

A minute later the autopilot was disengaged, followed by Al-Batouti again saying: "I rely on God."

Three seconds later, both engine throttles were reduced to zero and the elevators were moved 3 degrees, nosing the aircraft down. Six more times First-Officer Al-Batouti repeated "I rely on God" before the captain burst into the cockpit, demanding, "What's happening?"[2]

The flight data recorders suggest that the captain may have grasped the controls and commanded the nose up, while Al-Batouti commanded a nose down, at the same time that the engines were shut down.

The captain was heard demanding in a panicked voice: "What is this? Did you shut the engines?"

After an apparent struggle to take control of the aircraft, the left engine was torn from the wing by the extreme stress of the aircraft's maneuvers. Less than a minute later Flight 990 plummeted into the icy Atlantic, killing everyone on board.

In the aftermath of Flight 990's crash, in what could only be described as a further bizarre twist, Egyptian investigators concluded that their aircraft crashed solely as a result of mechanical failure. They chose to ignore all the pointed evidence from the cockpit voice recorder and the aircraft's flight data recorders—contained in the black boxes—data which indisputably pointed to suicide-by-pilot.

The US NTSB investigation, however, was published on March 21, 2002, after an eighteen month investigation, and this is their conclusion:

"The National Transportation Safety Board determines that the probable cause of the Egypt Air Flight 990 accident is the airplane's departure from normal cruise flight and subsequent impact with the Atlantic Ocean as a result of the relief first officer's flight control inputs. The reason for the relief first officer's actions was not determined."

Despite the glaring evidence in the NTSB's possession, the essence of the report appears watered down. By then, post 9/11, Egypt was an important ally in the war against the 'Axis of evil.' The US did not wish to overly offend its cordial relations with Egypt. Blame was laid at the first officer's door but there was certainly some watering down of the report, no doubt deemed necessary for the Egyptians to save face.

In fact, Egypt's ECAA final report, based largely on the NTSB's, came to an entirely different conclusion from precisely the *same* data:

'The Relief First Officer…did not deliberately dive the airplane into the ocean. Nowhere in the 1,665 pages of the NTSB's document or in the eighteen months of investigation effort is there any evidence to support the so called "deliberate act theory". In fact, the record contains specific evidence refuting such a theory, including an expert evaluation by Dr. Adel Fouad, a highly experienced psychiatrist.'

The Egyptians continue to lay the blame upon mechanical failure, a truly bizarre conclusion considering the NTSB evidence.

In search of a motive for Al-Batouti's behavior, international media reports suggested that he been reprimanded for sexual harassment—a serious charge within the Moslem airline. The reprimand had been made by Al-Batouti's boss, who happened to be on board the doomed plane.

But no mention was made in Egyptian newspapers at the time of the sexual harassment accusations against Al-Batouti.

One can only guess at the reasons for the illogical stance taken by the Egyptian authorities. National pride was perhaps at stake. And there exists a strong cultural aversion to suicide in Egypt. The country's tourist sector, vital to the economy and served by Egypt Air, would have suffered a serious blow had it been revealed immediately post 9/11 that one of their pilots was responsible for flying an Egypt Air aircraft into the ocean, dooming all its passengers

The point is, all the evidence indicates a pilot who deliberately crashed his aircraft by reason of suicide—on the evidence, no other conclusion really stood a chance. Yet vital reports by accident investigators whose duty it was to expose the exact reasons for the crash of Flight 990, deliberately watered down and molded the report to suit the politics of the day, and in the case of Egypt's ECAA, they almost totally ignored the facts.

Further disturbing acts earned Al-Batouti a severe reprimand from the senior captain on board Flight 990.

And yet despite such troubling behavior, Al-Batouti was still allowed take lone control of an airliner with 217 passengers on board.

The Federal Aviation Administration requires that US commercial pilots pass rigorous physical examination every six months if they are over 40 years old; yearly if under, as well as an assessment of their emotional stability.

The failure rate is low. In the US, for every 1,000 pilots tested, only two are denied certification for psychoneurotic disorders. Such pilots are grounded until they can pass the examination, if ever.

Around the world, mental health is a taboo issue, so it is with aviation. Pilots run a mile from any mention of the word; any hint of the illness can end your flying career. Enough to deter any pilot who may think there is a problem brewing.

David Powell of the Occupational and Aviation Medicine Unit at Otago University in Wellington, New Zealand, thinks aviation is going in the wrong direction when it comes to mental health. 'Depression is common and treatable, so surely the best way to manage it in aviation is to bring it out of hiding,' he says.

However, just as no security is fool proof, neither is any examination or test.

*

The most notorious suicide flights were carried out by men with basic flying skills while one, Hani Hanjour, had a commercial pilot's license. In the 9/11 attacks, Al Qaeda terrorists penetrated airport security and managed to hijack four US aircraft. The rest is an infamous blot on history.

As any air passenger can attest to, since 9/11 rigorous security has been enforced in airports worldwide. And yet deadly terrorist incidents still occur.

On Dec 25, 2009, Umar Farouk Abdulmutallab, a Nigerian national with an Al Qaeda connection, attempted to blow up Northwest Airlines Flight 253 travelling from Amsterdam to Detroit with 290 people on board. Abdulmutallab had sewn plastic explosives into his underwear. The device—a binary chemical bomb and 'a weapon of mass destruction' according to the FBI charge sheet—failed to detonate properly as the aircraft approached Detroit. The terrorist's clothes were set on fire in the attempt and a Dutch passenger, Jasper Schuringa, tackled and restrained him as other passengers helped put out the blaze, which in itself had the potential to cause serious havoc and damage on board.

This incident had the capacity to cause mass death and destruction but failed because of the clumsy attempts of the terrorist and the quick actions of passengers and crew. But terrorists learn from their mistakes.

In the words of one security expert, Johannes Beck, 'There are always cracks in a suit of armor. A terrorist only has to succeed once but security or counter-terrorist agencies whose task it is to prevent the terrorists have to succeed all the time.'

There are no reasons to believe that terrorist attacks will not continue, despite added and increased measures to counter it. Terrorists will simply try to find new ways to overcome the counter-measures.

The dissolution of Al Qaeda, like the dissolution of the PLO, may create a whole constellation of new and determined terror groups whose focus will be to hit western interests, and that especially includes aviation targets, because such incidents target large numbers of innocent civilians and create such a high media profile.

The Achilles' heel of the airline business is its regular schedules and its massive volume of passengers. In an effort to stem further binary bomb attacks such as the December 25th incident, full-body scanners are to be introduced into major international airports.

But as security expert Beck adds, 'Body scanners of themselves are not going to end the terrorist threat. The terrorists will simply discover more devious and clever ways of trying to hijack or destroy an aircraft. Body scanners may put an extra barrier in their path but the terrorist will eventually find a way of overcoming that additional barrier, and any other that is put in their path.'

The truth is, any security tends to be reactive, in that it often shifts up a gear or two or alters its focus after the event: listen to the media reports in the aftermath of an incident or attack and you'll hear the oft-quoted 'Passengers face even tighter security and longer delays at international airports after today's terrorist threat…'

How much tighter can you make already tight security?

Obviously it wasn't watertight to begin with.

The terrorist threat is also one of the major concerns of the International Federation of Airline Pilots Association, the umbrella group which represents pilots worldwide. The US body, ALPA International, which was successful in pushing for passenger screening in the 70's recently produced a white paper on this threat.

'A profoundly important gift was given to commercial aviation on Christmas Day 2009 when a failed terrorist attack against Northwest Flight 253 provided a wake-up call. We were reminded yet again, that highly determined radicals and extremists continue to plot new and different ways to inflict great economic harm on an airline industry which has yet to fully recover from the staggering costs inflicted on September 11, 2001.'

With such concerns in mind, it may make you wonder what kind of man or woman would want to face a potentially hostile work environment in which they also have to strap themselves into a cockpit seat and go hurtling through the air at hundreds of miles per hour in an aluminum tube?

Not only have they the growing threat of an act of terrorism on board their airliner to contend with, but on a daily basis pilots have to face technical catastrophes, a raft of security issues, longer flying hours, and the possible danger of inclement weather— weather which it seems is growing even more severe perhaps due to global warming.

What kind of man or woman is prepared to face such challenges daily?

What makes them possess 'the right stuff'?

What kind of training do they incur?

And last but not least, what are their own fears and concerns within a rapidly expanding aviation industry? Pilots are battling against an increasingly competitive and ruthless industry where the safety envelope is not only being pushed but ignored.

We will attempt to answer these questions in the next chapters. And some of the answers may well surprise and frighten you.

Chapter 5

The Right Stuff

What Makes a Safe Pilot?

'We're going to be in the Hudson.' Captain Chesley 'Sully' Sullenberger, responding to air traffic controllers asking on which runway he preferred to land US Airways Flight 1549. Jan. 15 2009

Aviators come from countless backgrounds. They have personal quirks like everyone else, but you can generalize when it comes to the basic characteristics of a pilot. There are certain traits that must be present.

Above all, pilots have to be quick-thinking survivors. They continually assess what they have done and they ask themselves if what they have done is working.

No matter what happens they cannot shrug their shoulders and simply give up.

Over and over, cockpit voice recorders have entombed the last challenging words of crews in disastrous situations who fought to the bitter end to regain control of a stricken aircraft.

In business a common and frustrating response is 'Okay, leave this problem with me. I'll get back to you.'

Seconds To Disaster

29

Pilots don't have that luxury.

They consistently have to assess a problem and often act within *seconds*. And it may not be a minor problem—regularly it is one that will decide the fate of hundreds of passengers.

The aviation industry demands that pilots stick to standard operating procedures— these are the procedures enshrined in aircraft manuals which flight crews are expected to follow to the letter, especially in the case of emergencies—yet US Federal Aviation Administration's chief scientific and technical adviser Dr Kathy Abbott believes that as much as 30% of aircraft failures were not foreseen by systems designers and so there were no checklists for them.

So it's obvious that there are times when the men and women in the cockpit have to be the kind of people who are not only capable of adhering to standard operating procedures, but if standard procedures fail and they are faced with a life or death situation then they also have to be capable of being able to think *outside* the box.

There are other qualities pilots must possess.

Whatever they think of life outside of work, once pilots are seated in the cockpit they have to be *absolute* positive thinkers. When muck hits the fan they must keep cool, work out not only how to avoid a mess but often they must also figure out what has caused it.

The only way to instill this instinct even further is to practice life-saving in a simulator.

A captain is normally teamed up with a first officer and over two days they act as a crew while the examiner throws disaster scenarios at them. They must turn these situations into manageable problems whether they are engine fires, systems failures, flight-control malfunctions, or any combination of failure and malfunction—whatever an instructor throws at them. Security and dangerous goods threats are simulated too.

They must pass these checks or face re-examination, training or loss of license. Pilots face losing their jobs in this way every six months.

But do pilots get enough training? This question was addressed in the US Airline Pilot's White paper report of September 2009 and the resulting testimony was—**they do not.** [3] However, the industry and its regulators do not always listen to such testimony by experienced aviators, but sometimes totally disregard it.

As with the flight crew of the influential Colgan Air disaster of February 2009, which will be examined in Chapter 11, we will see dangerous aviation industry practices exposed, in which air crews receive insufficient training.

In some cases such dangerous practices have been in existence for over six decades and put the lives of millions of unknowing passengers at risk. Training can sometimes fall seriously short due to time restrictions, both in the simulator or due to management cost-cutting or regulatory failings.

Readers will no doubt be aware of the heroic efforts of Captain Chesley 'Sully' Sullenberger. It is amazing how Captain Sullenberger managed to ditch his Airbus A320 in the Hudson successfully.

Any pilot you'd care to speak to was also totally amazed.

Not because they are less skilled - some are more some are less, and not because they thought they could never have done the same. But because contrary to belief, airline pilots, unlike some helicopter pilots, **do not** practice ditching in water.

However, along with flight attendants, pilots do practice the aftermath of a ditching at least once in a swimming pool.

But it may surprise some readers to know that there is currently no simulator software for landing on water, and no real life training scenario in how to ditch a plane. To be fair, it would be a difficult situation to reproduce.

In the aftermath of the Hudson Miracle, however, the US National Transportation Safety Board, NTSB, slated the industry's lack of training for this type of accident.

As well as the stresses outlined above, there are the myriad pressures of the actual work, of piloting an aircraft often with hundreds of passengers on board, and the daily regime of preparation for a flight.

Because flying airplanes for a living is not an industry for introverts, the operations room of an airline where pilots report for work and prepare flights can be a unique place.

On day five of a week of early 5 a.m. reports it's not easy to arrive at that hour of the morning and brighten the long day to come with a handshake and a smile. There are grunts, nods, baggy eyes. A short-lived caffeine induced alertness.

Pilots on check flights or who are on their way to becoming captains may well have been there an hour earlier to prepare. Schedules can be tough; this is not work for the faint hearted. Preparation means they must gather the paperwork, check it all, plan perhaps four legs—a leg being a complete one-way flight between two airports—and fill in the paperwork blanks. They will look at the predicted weather, airport notices and the condition of the aircraft offered to them for that day's work. (It's at this stage the pilots hope to detect any errors made earlier by flight planners and to catch something hidden among the paperwork, that may indicate problems ahead.)

They must then travel across the airport to their aircraft, check it during a visual inspection, complete safety and security checks; and— if time allows—brief the flight attendants. As well as that they must program the flight management computers for the flight ahead, check the maintenance logs, input the flight details, and deal with passenger boarding or cargo issues, airport delays and technical faults if any.

Some airlines allow just *forty-five minutes* from the pilot checking in for work to completing all the above. Others may require ultra-fast turnaround times—of 20 minutes, between the aircraft arriving on stand to pushing back with a new full load of passengers.

Tired already?

As for the men and women who find themselves gripped by a passion to fly and who will barter house and home to do it, they are in for a shock.

The cost of a commercial license, plus add-ons, continues to rise towards 130,000 US Dollars. A year-and-a-half in fulltime study, including weekends, is not the end of it.

Neither is the initial expense.

Pilots increasingly have to pay for the aircraft type rating, at least another thirty thousand dollars for a job that may pay you half that.

Having the 'right stuff' used to mean the pilot who had a combination of the requisite character traits for the job, coupled with a love of flying. These days the right stuff may simply mean having a large check book and little else to spend it on.

It may also mean having to enter the world of the Pay-To-Fly pilot because pilots must get experience, somewhere, somehow. They can pay thirty thousand dollars or more for the privilege of gaining experience on passenger carrying jet aircraft over a period of perhaps six months.

There is no way to avoid 'beginners' flying on the line with training captains and in this case, a safety pilot, is usually carried until the training captain is happy that in the event of his incapacitation the 'Trainee' could land the airplane safely. The problem with the Pay-To-Fly pilot system is that in many cases there is a **high turnover** of inexperienced pilots sitting in the right hand seat as co-pilot with fare-paying passengers on board.

Yes, you read it correctly. You, the passenger, sometimes fly with rookie pilots who are paying for the privilege of sitting in that seat. And this brings us to some other disturbing revelations that the flying public ought to know.

Chapter 6

Lethal Airlines

When it's Safer Not to Fly

'I once sat as a concerned passenger in an aircraft about to taxi on the runway at Moscow's Sheremetyevo airport, while a snowstorm was blowing and witnessed two mechanics try to beat the crap out of a badly-fitting metal engine cowl as they attempted to fit it into place with blows from their rubber mallets. Much to my disappointment, they eventually succeeded.

As I called the flight attendant to voice my concern, the aircraft promptly took off. Safely, which seemed to me like a miracle. But twenty minutes into the flight the attendant came round with the drinks trolley and handed me a Styrofoam cup for my drink. Around the rim I saw lipstick and the clear outline of teeth marks. I was on the flight from hell...'

The list of airlines banned from flying within European airspace is long enough to fill **26 pages**.[4] List of airlines banned within the EU.

The US regulator, the FAA, has a list of zones or states which are 'unapproved.' Airlines from those areas or states are forbidden from entering US airspace but, incredibly, the FAA will not specify the airlines, which is not much use to you, the fare-paying passenger, as you plan your travel abroad.

35

The European agency, however, regularly updates the list and tells you outright the names of the companies they say are not up to standard.

There are thousands of airlines around the world, but some in fact are not real airlines and are known in the industry as Virtual Airlines. They hire or outsource planes and crews from other companies.

Flight Global, a leader in aviation comment, has this to say on the virtual airline phenomenon: 'Commercial air transport operators provide a unique kind of service. They should not be treated, in law, like companies that sell tickets for, say, theatre seats. At no stage before, during or after a theatre performance does the audience find their seats collectively careering at nearly 300km/h along a short tarmac path in a three-wheeled vehicle that was not designed to operate on the ground, before being launched into the sky. Neither do theatre-goers contract to spend several hours in an artificially pressurized container traversing the troposphere at 750km/h before being aimed at another small tarmac strip to impact with it at some 250km/h'.

To pursue the theatrical analogy, a virtual carrier may be nothing more than a ticket agency.

Flight Global believe virtual airlines should be a thing of the past. 'What really provides safety in an airline is unbroken lines of responsibility and control, a corporate ethos, and a set of company standard operating procedures. A ticket agency that contracts out its customers to three or four different operators all with different aircraft types cannot offer the standards that passengers expect when they purchase an airline ticket.'[5]

Another worrying development is that many airlines are now challenging the captain's authority onboard his aircraft, to prevent him making safety decision that may cost them money. Pilots are appearing in court or finding themselves in difficult employment circumstances for making safety decisions that did not ring well with management. For instance, a diversion for safety reasons to an alternative airport can be costly for an airline, as can delaying boarding over re-fueling safety concerns.

Airlines may also ban pilots from being members of unions or pilot associations, but in aviation terms, these associations can be the last line of defense for safety. Otherwise pilots do not have any protection against attempts from commercially driven or ill-informed managements to push pilots into actions that go against their professional judgment.'[6]

US Airways, the airline employing the Miracle on the Hudson River pilots, are not immune to problems. A recent audit by Illumia, University of Illinois, found the safety culture there is poor and 'has led to cutting corners'. Management have dismissed the report. "In summary, the results of the survey indicate that US Airways' Flight Operations has a negative safety culture, with some areas driven by a fixed, unyielding view from leadership, and others reflective of employees feeling they must take safety matters into their own hands."[7]

In the words of Tom Kubik, safety committee chairman, USAPA, 'a poor safety culture will inevitably affect the safety record.'[8]

Captain Chesley Sullenberger and First Officer Jeffrey Skiles, the crew who successfully ditched their dying Airbus A320 in the Hudson River in New York have not hesitated in speaking out about the concerns they have about their own airline.

'The success of Flight 1549 was due to the professionalism, experience and dedication to safety of the US Airways employee groups, especially the pilots and flight attendants. This has been **in spite of** US Airways management, not because of it. The continued safety of our passengers requires that US Airways management establish a genuine commitment to safety and create an effective safety culture in partnership with the employee groups. We commend US Airways employees for maintaining their focus on passenger safety, despite Management's lack of leadership, their attacks on Captain's authority, and their creation of a flawed safety culture,' said Sully Sullenberger and Jeffrey Skiles.

Harsh words indeed. Meanwhile passengers strap into their seats, completely unaware that the pilots in whom they place their trust are increasingly finding themselves stuck between a rock and a hard place. Should they satisfy management demands by pushing the safety margin, or just say no and risk losing their job? Confident pilots, who are backed up by a union or association are not so vulnerable to these pressures. But as we will now see, even pilots who do have this backing are finding they are just too disheartened or brow-beaten to make those kinds of calls when it matters most.

*

'In my private life I've been drunk and I've been fatigued, they both feel very similar, both have debilitating effects. I've only experienced one of them on the flight deck, fatigue and I might as well have been drunk.' Airline training captain.

Glenn Meade/Ray Ronan

A peculiar word, fatigue; it suggests many things to many people and is easily dismissed by skeptics. It's a condition that is difficult to prove even when a fatigued patient presents himself to a medical practitioner; it's easy to see how it could escape reference in an aviation accident or serious incident. Despite this, fatigue is considered by air accident investigators to be a factor in 20% of airline accidents, a figure often disputed by airlines.

Safety is said to be the number one priority at every airline, but not all pilots believe this is true of the company they work for. 'Over the last three years cost has been the overriding focus of the business,' says one captain.

Fatigue may be a dirty word in aviation but many pilots will maintain it is at an all time high, and that 'it has just become part of our work.'.[9]

To minimize risk many airlines use fatigue management systems to monitor pilot work rosters. But such systems are not always adhered to or can be flawed. Some airlines do not even recognize fatigue as a problem. For pilots, this often means they are being pushed to the limits.

A commercial airline captain with a major low fares airline talks about how his constant tiredness is affecting the standard of training he provides his trainee pilots. 'I don't bother thinking anymore; I just know I'm too tired to bother with it. I know I made several mistakes during my last simulator session, I'm pretty sure the crew may have failed an item, but I have no idea what they did. I was just too tired to care.'[10]

Too many crew—including flight attendants,—are afraid to call in sick for fear of losing their jobs.

Flying when ill debilitates a crewmember's ability to make safe decisions; it also adds to fatigue levels. A fatigued/distracted pilot is a short step away from failing in his duties altogether.

UCL, University College London conducted a survey of pilots at one airline.[11] The survey found pilots often flew right up to the maximum safe level of hours , and flew above and beyond the *recommended* safe limit of work hours in a day at least **24** times a year. Levels of fatigue, sleep problems, levels of anxiety, and depression, were higher than would be expected in a general population. The survey also found and discussed poor mental health among the pilots.[12] Results such as these ought to ring alarm bells worldwide for airline passengers.

In the Colgan Air crash of 2009 in Buffalo, 50 were people killed. Fatigue induced by long commutes for the pilots were cited as contributing towards the accident.[13]   In 2010, an Air India Boeing 737 overshot the runway, fell over a cliff and a fire ensued among the wreckage. 158 died. Fatigue was cited as a key factor in the crash.[14]

In the US, new flight duty time rules set by the FAA in late 2011 don't go far enough. 'I'm very distressed over these rules,' John Nance, a former Air Force and Airline pilot told NBC news, 'because they don't go anywhere near far enough and they bear the earmarks of having listened to the whining of the airline industry. We have needed comprehensive change in our duty time controls for fatigue for a long time and this just ignores about 25 years of research.'[15]

Strong lobbying by airlines to allow pilots to work long hours continues to have an influence, this despite scientific studies that advise otherwise. It demands lobbying by pilot groups who must journey to DC in an attempt to counter the powerful aviation representatives. A pilots' group study suggests that 50% of the pilot sample are over the threshold for sleep disorders.[16]

If a pilot kills you due to pilot error caused by fatigue, he will doubtless be blamed.

And yet the airline he worked for will be well within its right to hold up its hand and say, 'But it was legal…'

Chapter 7

Improper Maintenance

When Good Enough Just Isn't Good Enough

On December 20 1995, American Airlines flight 965 lay scattered on a mountainside near Cali, Columbia. While bodies still lay on the ground, helicopters flying in rescuers took away engine thrust reversers, cockpit avionics, even landing gear from the Boeing 757. American Airlines were forced to publish the serial numbers of all the missing items, revealing for the first time the extent of a dark industry; black market aircraft parts.

Aircraft from the US routinely fly to South America or Asia for heavy maintenance, and the cost savings can be in the millions. Already highly successful unapproved parts dealers can take further advantage of the outsourcing of maintenance by airlines to the far-flung reaches of the world.

Nobody, it seems, is immune to the problem. NASA's Keppler spacecraft, now investigating the depths of our solar system, was found to contain an unspecified counterfeit part; a nine month launch delay ensued. NASA have been tackling this problem for years. 'We often find out late they are counterfeit parts,' says Christopher Scolese, who at the time was the space agency's acting administrator. 'We find out about it while (the part is) sitting atop a rocket or, worse, when the rocket is in space.'[1]

Seconds To Disaster

43

The US military believe there may be up to 80 percent infiltration of counterfeit parts in its inventory. [2] Some have even found their way onto the United States President's own aircraft, Air Force One.

If these United States' institutions cannot contain the problem, what hope has a passenger aircraft that may be sitting in an unsecured maintenance facility?

A simple, sturdy metal bolt may ordinarily cost a few dollars or less. But if destined for use in an aircraft a specialized metal bolt may cost a hundred times more; it will likely have to be manufactured to exceptionally high tolerances, and be incredibly durable, able to tolerate extremes of temperature and stress. The motive for those for involved in illicitly manufacturing and supplying fake aircraft parts is simple: profit. But often these parts fail, with catastrophic results.

September 8th, 1989. Partnair Flight 394 was flying at 20,000 feet off the Danish coast. Counterfeit bolts failed causing the tail section to tear off. All 55 people onboard died.

Black market spares litter the inventories of airlines and maintenance companies all over the world, but airlines will often not discuss the issue in public. So no-one knows the true scale of the counterfeit—or unapproved parts—problem.

Outsourcing of aircraft maintenance by airlines, on occasion to remote or unfamiliar facilities that they have not previously used, has been known to sometimes increase the risk of these counterfeit items finding their way onto planes. It can also impede the ability of regulators to check the source of parts.

The unapproved, rehashed or counterfeit spares are almost always accompanied by professionally produced false paperwork and labels designed to fool maintenance staff.

Counterfeiters are becoming increasingly sophisticated, often using laser etching of actual parts themselves to create manufacturers markings and serial numbers. Because aircraft spares are incredibly expensive, and in the case of older aircraft hard to source, the black-market in aviation spares is highly profitable. One head of a counterfeit parts ring said she had moved on from distributing drugs to aircraft parts, simply because it was much more lucrative.

It is estimated the trade in suspected unapproved parts, known as SUP's, could be billions of dollars annually. The FAA estimates 520,000 counterfeit parts are used each year. These parts do not comply with quality controls, may likely not be within strict manufacturing tolerances, and may not be up to the job. If they are used in a critical part of the aircraft, they may likely kill.

On June 19th, 1995 an engine exploded on a ValuJet DC-9. Shrapnel slashed through the aircraft, a cabin fire ensued, and passengers and crew were injured.

Unapproved maintenance at a Turkish facility was cited.[3]

But aircraft parts are not the only 'fake' problem. Unskilled or untrained personnel are repairing and servicing aircraft.

Resource stretched FAA inspectors who did manage to inspect outsource facilities have discovered insufficiently trained or unqualified personnel working on aircraft. Even pilot licenses have been added to the counterfeit problem: in 2010 the Civil Aviation Authority of the Philippines asked the National Bureau of Investigation to look into the proliferation of fake licenses.'[4]

US airline companies are fined every year for failing to carry out vital aircraft maintenance or for not implementing safety recommendations. These practices put millions of lives in mortal danger.

Pushing the limits of their aircraft is one way for a cash strapped airline to save money. Swapping parts from one plane to another to avoid replacement limits; disregarding maintenance schedules and failing to adhere to regulators and manufacturers regulations are other surreptitious ways of saving money. Many airlines delay replacing faulty parts until 'the last possible date.'

In doing so it affects aircraft safety.

In 2003 A British Airways 757 had serious flight control problems after departure from London Heathrow; engine oil smoke was also invading the cockpit. The problems occurred *after* the aircraft had returned from maintenance. 'Ineffective supervision of maintenance staff had allowed working practices to develop that had compromised the level of airworthiness control, and had become accepted as the norm,' said investigators. [5]

Compromise seems to happen more and more often in the aviation industry. As one seasoned contract aircraft engineer recently remarked: 'I asked a new engineer to inspect an aircraft's aileron. (A critical control surface that affects the aircraft's banking movement) He gave me puzzled look and told me that he didn't know what an aileron was.'[6]

Aircraft maintenance used to be carried out by fully qualified mechanics. Now it's cheaper to have only one trained aircraft mechanic designated as a supervisor, while the other maintenance staff are trained to work on one system only such as landing gear, or hydraulic systems, and are paid much less than their previously fully qualified colleagues. Generally, one supervisor must check the work of up to a dozen or more of these 'specialists'.

Modern aircraft are complicated pieces of equipment, and the irony is that the more automated they become, the more interdependent all those systems become upon one another. When a specialist does not fully understand the repercussions of one system on another, this creates the chance for error.

Errors, even minor ones, are found at the birthplace of all disasters.

An Alaska airlines MD80 fell into the Pacific Ocean on January 31, 2000 after a large control surface at the rear of the jet flopped uselessly due to lack of lubrication on a screw. 88 people died; poor maintenance at Alaska Airlines was cited in the NTSB air Accident report.

In 1985, what remains as the largest single aircraft fatal accident, occurred when Japan Airlines Flight 123 crashed due to poor maintenance—520 people died. Improper rear bulkhead repairs were blamed.

Maintenance cost-cutting and poor regulatory control puts passengers and crew at risk every day, and as airlines fight to survive it becomes an increasing problem.

174 US Aircraft crashes and incidents over a ten year period are attributed to counterfeit parts. Do cutbacks in maintenance and the shortcomings in supervision allow this danger to grow?

AIA, the Aerospace Industries Association, has a game plan which attempts to start tackling this issue, but if governments are serious about this they first need to recognize how big a problem it is.

James Frisbee was a quality control chief at Northwest Airlines, 'It's very, very hard to pin the cause of an accident on a part that failed ... especially when the airplane is scattered over five acres.'

Chapter 8

Children and Airline Safety

Aviation's Second Class Safety for children

"You told me to put my son on the floor, I did, and he's gone," a passenger on United Airlines Flight 232 told Flight Attendant Jan Brown after the plane crashed killing 111 passengers.[1]

Commercial jets—designed to withstand incredible stresses during flight caused by storms, wayward jet streams or wake turbulence—have sometimes limped home having protected their passengers through terrifying flight conditions.[2]
From time to time, runway excursions occur with the aircraft running into the dirt, slamming to a halt, but staying intact and in doing so have safeguarded their occupants.

Secured to the floor of those aircraft are the seats, designed to withstand severe movements and impacts which could increase your weight by up to 16 times. Passengers are strapped in by a lap belt that fastens them down using the sides of the pelvis as an anchor to keep them safe and secure: unless you are an infant or a child.

Aircraft seats and their lap belts are designed for adults; they offer no protection for children or infants. In automobiles, children are not allowed to travel with just a lap belt.

Seconds To Disaster

Yet airlines are allowed to provide children with nothing. Why?

Let's start with the child. Up to about age 7, the pelvis, which the lap belt uses to secure you into your seat, is not fully developed. 'In the course of an accident, the belt slips completely into the abdominal region which leads to severe internal injuries,' says a report from TÜV,[3] a company specializing in seat belt testing for many decades.

They detail how the current seat belt length is designed so the buckle sits in the middle of the adult waist; on a child it sits to the side and often with the lap belt remaining loose. 'Due to the lateral position of the lift-lever buckle, a life-threatening fracture can be caused.'

The report also tells how a loose belt places additional loads on the child during a violent stop. Videos of crash testing show the upper part of the child's body jack-knifing forward, the head striking the arms and legs before the forehead actually manages to hit the front of the very seat the child is sitting on and striking its metal structure. Infants fare even worse.

This poses a serious question: is serious or fatal injury of a child or infant not only possible but likely in the event of a survivable aircraft accident?

The situation is bad for children worldwide. If you board an aircraft in Europe or Australia with a child under 2 years old, you will be handed a loop belt.

The infant sits on your lap while you push your seatbelt through the small loop and you feel they are safe. Airlines will insist you use it. You have no choice unless the airline allows approved child seats.

Glenn Meade/Ray Ronan

The TÜV report describes what happens to an infant secured with a loop belt in the event of a crash or survivable accident. The loop belt is lethal—it doesn't stop until it crushes up against the spine of the infant. You can only imagine what has happened to all those vital organs, all that soft tissue in the stomach. [4] TÜV explains: 'the infant acts as an energy absorption element.' To be blunt, an infant secured to the lap with a loop belt becomes a human airbag for the adult.

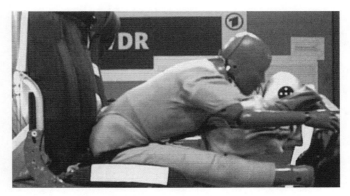

Testing at TÜV. Note the position of the child's loopbel against the spine.
Photo Courtesy of Tim Van Beveren.

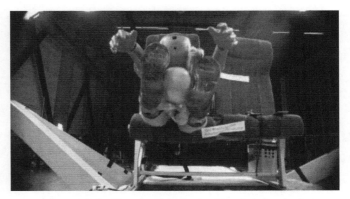

Testing at TÜV. Note the adult's head striking the infants head.
Photo Courtesy of Tim Van Beveren.

Seconds To Disaster

Some airlines allow you to use an approved car seat, or the Cares system.[5]

Some do not. It's likely that the flight attendants on your trip will be unsure about when and how they can be used, and may argue that they may not be used at all. The whole system is a shameful, dangerous mess, often perpetuated by airlines worldwide. Children and infants are denied proper safety in flight for the sake of a few dollars in cost saving.

In common with pilots and safety experts worldwide, Tim Van Beveren, aviation investigative journalist for more than 20 years, cannot understand why this loop belt is still in use. [6]

He asked Martin Sperber of TÜV the same question during the filming of a documentary on airline passenger safety (see still pictures, this chapter). Sperber replied: 'I don't know... (the loop belt) is not an approved restraining system for children, it was designed to prevent children from 'missiling' through the cabin and thereby injuring other passengers.

Our test results are known for more than a decade, yet they are simply ignored.'[7]

These examples show you the forces that are at work during an emergency, or even during severe turbulence. So what if your child is not restrained at all?

On US or a US registered aircraft, the loop belt is banned by the FAA. You will be refused carriage on the flight and perhaps arrested if you refuse to put on your seatbelt as it's required by law as stated by the FAA - 'To keep you and your family as safe as possible during flight, FAA regulations require passengers to be seated with their seat belts fastened:

Glenn Meade/Ray Ronan

- When the airplane leaves the gate and as it climbs after take-off.
- During landing and taxi.
- Whenever the seat belt sign is illuminated during flight.'

Yet they only 'recommend' children are restrained, leaving it up to the parents and the airline to figure it out.[8] Most airlines don't bother to provide safe transport and yet still charge you to hold a child on your lap where they are unsecured and completely vulnerable to danger.

"A safety seat is the safest place for your child—and the way you can be sure to hold on to her for a lifetime,"[9] says an FAA radio advertisement encouraging *parents* to provide safe air travel for their child, something they are reluctant to force the airlines to do while absolving themselves of all responsibility.

For over 30 years, the NTSB[10] has investigated aircraft accidents involving unrestrained children and has issued safety recommendations that have been ignored. 'We all see it regularly when we travel, parents putting their children in child safety seats when they drive to the airport and checking the car seat in with their luggage and then holding their child on their lap during the flight, even when everyone else on the plane is required to be buckled in. Once at their destination, they pick up their seat at the baggage claim and then they secure their child again on the car trip from the airport.'[11]

Your children may mean everything to you, but as chilling and callous as it sounds, 'children not allocated their own seat do not appear in listed victim numbers in airline crash statistics.'[12]

TÜV believe the use of Child Restraint Systems in aircraft causes additional costs to the airlines. Is this simple cost why regulators are failing our children?

It's an argument airlines often used against installing terrain warning equipment, weather radar or traffic avoidance systems on board aircraft. These now mandatory enhancements have since saved countless lives.

Child safety-seats designed and approved for aircraft are available and in use by government bodies on VIP and military transport. Innovint Aircraft Interior's in Hamburg, Germany, showed us their 'SkyKids child seat', easy to use, quick to fit and can be rear or forward facing. The seat has been taken up a handful of airlines. Hainan - China, Tam - Brazil and Air Mauritius.

In the words of Manfred Gröning, CEO of Innovint: '911 was a tragedy in so many ways, but one victim was child safety in aviation. The issue was coming to a head and it seemed vital changes were about to take place. Then 911 happened and child safety priority was chopped.'

The Swiss Air-Ambulance service uses this seat to properly secure children on its Challenger jets. Maintanance manager Werner Schmid says: 'We felt we needed to secure children on our aircraft. This seat does it.'

Virgin Atlantic does have a seat and this is puts in place for you when you book a child fare, 'While your children enjoy their dedicated inflight entertainment, they'll be comfy and **safe** in our seats designed just for them.'[13]

Concerned parents of child passengers can go to the end of this book to find out what steps you can take when flying to make traveling in an aircraft safer for your child.

Glenn Meade/Ray Ronan

Meanwhile, safety advice and guidelines are all that the regulatory authorities the world over provide to an aviation industry whose primary aim is to make money. Each and every airline is left to decide what is best for our children's safety, and the result should leave the public in no doubt that safety is **not** the main priority of many airlines. If it was, every child would have a safe and secure seat.

Airlines and their regulators ignore children's safety by willful neglect.

Jan Brown was a flight attendant onboard United Airlines Flight 232 on July 19, 1989, when her DC-10 crashed in Sioux City.

The cabin was prepared, with everything secured for the emergency, but not the infants who were either held in their parent's arms or were placed on the floor. 22-month-old Evan was one of those infants. He died. Jan has since battled for child safety.

"At the time that was all we had, but it was far from what we should have had for the protection of those children. No parent should find out in this way that holding a child on a lap is unsafe."

More than 2 decades later, there is still no regulation forcing airlines to provide safe seating for infants and children. Jan Brown adds: "When preparing the cabin for an emergency, flight attendants should not have to look a parent in the eye and instruct them to continue to hold the lap child when we know there is a very real possibility that child may not survive without proper restraints."

Is there evidence that children held on their parent's lap or placed on the floor are safe? No, but is there evidence that children are at risk? Yes.

This has been known as far back as Sept 1996, when three lap babies torn from parent's arms during turbulence were hospitalized on a Lufthansa flight over Texas. In December 1996 turbulence on an American Airlines flight saw a three-month-old baby hospitalized. No organization keeps track of how many children are injured or killed on flights.

"The fact that the FAA refuses to be bothered with rule-making remains egregious and totally irresponsible...focusing on airline profits rather than safety," says Brown, now a long term advocate of airline child safety.

Mary Schiavo, former Inspector General of the US Dept. of Transportation- "One FAA spokesperson is reported to have stated, 'There haven't been enough infants killed on airlines to justify changing, (the law).'[14]

Until regulators force the airlines to simply raise the safety level of infants and children to **the level enjoyed by adults**, most airlines will take the cheaper and most cost effective route, leaving your child's safety in the lap of the gods.

Chapter 9

The Elephant Nobody Wants to Talk About

Toxic Cabin

'This is aviation's best kept secret.'

John Hoyte, a Training Captain and Founder of Aerotoxic Association.

In 1993 international scientists from the US, France and Australia proposed that Aerotoxic Syndrome was responsible for the ill health of airline passengers and crew. In a rerun of the battle about smoking, the response from the airline industry is akin to the approach adopted by the tobacco industry which denied   the known harmful effects of smoking for years.

But what is Aerotoxic Syndrome and how is it caused?

In order to have a comfortable environment and sufficient air pressure to breathe at the altitudes at which jet airliners fly, a supply of warm compressed air is required.

This is supplied directly from the jet engines and is known as bleed air.

It is mixed inside the aircraft with re-circulated cabin air at a ratio of 50/50. Although some of the air is re-circulated, all of it originates from the jet engines.

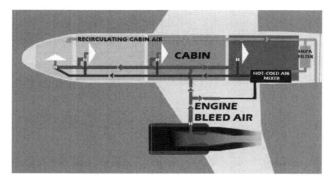

Typical Bleed Air System

But the air pumped in from the jet engines is not usually filtered, so there is a danger of contaminants reaching the passengers and crew in the cabin.

The seals between various parts of the engines are prone to wear, or poor maintenance. They cannot be 100% effective and fail from time to time. Numerous studies show that if they leak a little, trace amounts of oil fumes can escape into the bleed air on the way to the cabin.[15] But if the seals fail completely, large volumes of fumes can escape into the air conditioning system in what's now known in the aviation industry as a 'Fume Event.' The fumes contain a cocktail of dangerous chemicals. The UK government admits there is at least 1 fume event per 2000 flights.[16] That's 50,000 passengers and crew out of Heathrow alone per year involved in the *known* fume events.

A fume event on US Airways flight #432 from Phoenix,
Arizona to Maui, Hawaii on 17 September 2010. The airplane
was a B757. The flight was diverted to San Francisco.

If compounds are getting into the aircraft cabin, why are they so dangerous? 'Oils are complex and designed to withstand the extreme environment of the engines. TCP is an organophosphate (OP), and organophosphates were originally designed for their neurotoxic properties and used in the manufacture of pesticides and nerve agents,' says Hoyte, an ex-airline captain affected by contaminated aircraft cabin air.

Captain John Hoyte, Founder of Aerotoxic Association.

The inhalation of these dangerous fumes may cause what has become commonly referred as 'Aerotoxic Syndrome'.

'There is a growing body of evidence, globally, of compromised flight safety caused by oil fumes, as well as documentation for near-daily oil fume events on the US Airways fleet,' says Tom Kubik, Safety Chairman US Airways.

It is believed that US airways suffers one fume event per week.

And this may be just the tip of a very ugly iceberg. 'Aerospace physicians have pointed out that Flight Crew, as a cross section of society, suffer more neurological un-wellness than most of society and the highest rates of cancer,' says Captain David Zaharik of Air Canada, grounded due to TCP poisoning. 'Many pilots put it down to a side effect of the job, bad food, stress, jet lag.'

And perhaps passengers do too.

But why doesn't it affect everyone? Some scientists believe that, as with smoking, toxic compounds cause harm to some people more than others.[17]

This too is why some crewmembers suffer recognizable symptoms and some don't. Professor Jeremy Ramsden, a leading researcher into this issue believes passengers and crew should be educated to the risks of contaminated cabin air. 'Vulnerable people should be identified whenever possible and advised not to travel by jet airliners fitted with bleed air technology. Given that there is some evidence for reproductive toxicity of TCP, pregnant women should at least be made aware of the risk.'[18]

Not only do the airlines, regulators and manufacturers have to fight against the growing evidence of 'Fume Events', it also appears they will have to contend with the emergent belief that TCP's are present in cabin air, *most of the time.*

It is possible that people reading this are suffering from the same symptoms as John Hoyte, who was finally grounded in February 2006. 'Passengers have no reason to think their sickness may have its root cause on-board a commercial flight.' says Hoyte. 'Have you ever suffered 'jet lag' and simply not got over it for a long time? Light headedness, tinnitus, loss of balance? Shaking and tremors?'

But the effects go far beyond everyday symptoms that may be explained away. According to one of many experts exploring this issue, Professor Abou Donia, 'Exposed crewmembers were found to have brain damage and cell death.'[19]

David Learmount of Flight Global magazine believes Europeans are washing their hands of the problem.[20] 'They have strenuously avoided getting involved in the passenger and crew health aspects of bleed air contamination on the grounds that passenger and crew health is not their business.'[21] He is among many aviation experts who hope the growing number of prominent scientists working on the health effects of TCP poisoning will provide enough momentum to bring this to a conclusion. 'I wonder how many European passengers know that the aviation authorities say that passenger and crew health on board public transport airplanes is of no concern to them?'

Solutions are there in the form of organophosphate-free engine oils; fitting filters to lessen the effect; a system of sensors to alert crew to a fume event or using compressed air that does not come from the engines—such as on the new Boeing 787 Dreamliner.

It could take years, perhaps decades, to prove without doubt the health effects of contaminated cabin air.

'We prefer to follow the principle of precaution when a serious doubt is present. None of us want to be at the receiving end of a bio-chemical experiment,' say the Air Canada Pilots Association.

Chapter 10

Boeing's Problems

Broken Trust

'...sooner or later one of these aircraft will lose its ability to stay together... it will become a smoking hole in the ground.'

Former FAA official Dr Michael Dreikorn talking about the Boeing 737NG

The art of air travel demands that every passenger and crewmember must have complete faith in the system that ensures the integrity of every aspect of flight. Most of all, passengers and crew must have complete trust in the actual aircraft they fly.

What if that trust is broken by a world market leader in aircraft manufacturing, such as Boeing? As out of character and disturbing a claim as it appears, Boeing stands accused of doing just that.

Put simply, former managers at the Boeing plant claim that their company airframes, the skeletons of over 1500 of its aircraft—mainly the 737 NG— are not airworthy and should be grounded.

A Next Generation of Design.

In 1998 the much anticipated Boeing 737NG (Next Generation) rolled off the production line in a successful bid to compete with the high-tech Airbus A320.

Presented to the FAA as an aircraft designed and built by computer controlled machines, the parts produced were to fit together so well that there would be no gaps between airframe parts that normally require fillers; no manually drilled holes that reduce airframe strength. The metal would be cut to within 3000ths of an inch by extremely expensive computer controlled machines and tools, creating an aircraft with superior tolerances, elevated strength, and all at a lighter weight.

Based on the strict controls Boeing would put in place, the high precision of the tools it would use, and the plans submitted to the FAA for the aircraft's approval—Boeing's technological advances would allow the 737NG to carry more, to fly higher, and in doing so endure increased stresses.

However, according to Boeing employees, the aircraft that rolled off the production line during full production were *not* built to the same standard as the original prototype and *not* according to the approved manufacturing system.

Instead of parts interlocking seamlessly, hammers were used to make parts fit; out of alignment holes were redrilled and some cuts of metal were off by up to 2 inches—far from the 3000th of an inch approved by the FAA. Fillers *were* used and parts were hammered into place; which produced pre-stresses on metal not made for ill-treatment.

This occurred not to extraneous parts that simply fit onto the aircraft, but the parts that *make* the aircraft—Primary Structural Elements or PSE'S.

Here is an extract from Boeing's 737 repair manual:

<u>WARNING</u>: THE FAILURE OF PSE'S COULD RESULT IN THE CATASTROPHIC FAILURE OF THE AIRPLANE.

According to some experts, failure isn't a matter of if but when, and they believe it's already happening.

These ill-fitting parts, and un-approved parts, were not made by Boeing, but by a manufacturer called AHF Ducommun. If the parts produced by Ducommun with their computer controlled machines didn't fit, why not? How could they be so far off?

300 of the 737 NG aircraft were already in service by the time Boeing employee Gigi Prewit was promoted to purchasing manager of parts for that project.

Immediately, shop fitters alerted her to the ongoing problem of parts arriving that just did not fit. Prewit approached her managers and a team was sent in to investigate the parts manufacturer AHF Ducommun. What they found over a two week period at the manufacturer's plant horrified them. They took photographs, '...because nobody would believe us otherwise.'

The parts were being made not by the FAA approved process-using high tech machines-but by hand. Templates were used to draw parts with magic-markers which were then cut with handsaws and resized by belt sanders in a process reminiscent of cabinet makers in a carpentry workshop.

This not only violated the conditions of the aircraft design but the parts created were weakened and already stressed before being used to construct airframes in which passengers and crew were to sit for the next 30 years or more.

What followed is like something from a thriller novel. Threats against the investigating team by Ducommun were alleged: 'We have long arms that reach into Boeing, you will be shot...' 'We will shove 20 of your rejected parts up your....'

An email recommendation by the team to cease using Ducommun as a supplier stated that, 'continued trading...places the Boeing company at risk.' The email was deleted by Boeing management the following day.

The investigating team was told not to divulge any of their findings to anyone but Boeing management or face a law suit by Boeing.

Gigi Prewit and another employee, Taylor Smith, had to decide where their loyalties lay—with the safety of the public or with the company that employed them. In Gigi's case, her relatives had worked for Boeing for generations. It seemed that by now there were so many aircraft flying, that to admit there was a problem could bring about financial ruin for Boeing as the grounding of 300 Aircraft, or the forced ongoing inspection and maintenance required would precipitate fatal lawsuits from airline customers.

Despite warnings of legal action from Boeing, Prewit and Smith approached the Department of Justice who were initially horrified by the information. They ordered the FAA to investigate. Public documents show that the only investigation the FAA carried out was to look up the Ducommun website and note the address.

A criminal investigation by the Department of Defense found

there were non-conforming parts, saying that the forced fit of these parts at the Boeing plant could cause problems.

This was all very soon followed by an order from the US Department of Justice to cease all investigation into the issue.

Yet still the aircraft rolled off the lines, and flew, and carried passengers and crew at higher altitudes, at a higher weight.

Despite promises from the department of Justice to keep the whistleblowers' names secret, and to protect them, Boeing found out who they were.

Now they are out of work and unlikely to find any.

The first inkling that the Department of Justice was trying to protect Boeing was when the Department released a statement portraying the NTSB as having indicated that the breakup of a Boeing aircraft—an American Airlines 737NG that crash-landed in Jamaica on December 22nd, 2009—had nothing to do with the allegedly unapproved parts.

The NTSB denied making this statement.

And when Boeing lawyers began drafting statements for the Federal Aviation Administration to announce—for the very authority whose job it is to regulate Boeing—this put the whistleblowers in a very lonely place.

The still young 737 NG aircraft were suffering from fatigue, cracks and structural failures after only 8 years into a 30 year life.

Airlines and military operators of the aircraft are reporting (to the FAA) mounting problems with these aircraft.

Former FAA official Dr Michael Dreikorn is 'very seriously concerned about a catastrophic cabin failure at altitude,' that sooner or later one of these aircraft will lose its ability to stay together. He believes it will be a 737 NG and it will become, 'a smoking hole in the ground.'

The FAA says it does not believe there are any issues with the 737 NG. [1][2][3]

Other aircraft designs were allowed to fly even though technical problems persisted. For years, the Boeing 767 flew with its thrust reversers disabled after the Lauda Air disaster, in which the aircraft's reversers were inadvertently deployed by the plane's computers and caused a mid-air destruction of the Lauda Air aircraft, killing everyone on board.

Yet regulators still permitted that model aircraft to fly, even though the problem which caused a major disaster and loss of life had not yet been resolved. The decision by regulators put millions of passengers' lives at risk.

The reason? Pressure from airlines, which faced financial ruin in some cases, if a complete ban of flying the 767 was enforced. So a compromise was reached with regulators and the troublesome reverser was completely disabled on the 767 until a solution was found.

Powerful lobbying from airlines, and their priority of limiting costs despite the risk to passenger and crew safety, won out again in the end.

Chapter 11

The Critical Eleven Minutes

3 Minutes After Takeoff, 8 Minutes Before Landing

Colgan Flight 3407, one of the most influential air accidents in American aviation history.

The Colgan Air crash on February 12, 2009, occurred five miles out from Buffalo Niagara airport in up-state New York. Compared to any single accident since commercial aviation began it would have the most profound influence on aviation, and not solely in the United States.

Most aircraft accidents occur during what are called the 'Critical Eleven Minutes'—within three minutes after take-off, and eight minutes before landing. The loss of Colgan Air flight 3407 occurred during the approach phase of the Critical Eleven Minutes.

When aircraft fly high and fast they are aerodynamically 'clean'. However, during this eleven-minute period when an aircraft is taking off or landing, it flies slower and has what is termed a 'dirty' configuration. The aircraft is, of course, closer to the ground and any obstacles surrounding the airport.

On takeoff, flaps and slats are pushed out to the front and rear of the wing, making the wing surface larger and increasing lift at the aircraft's low speeds.

On approach to landing, spoilers may be pushed up on top of the wings to 'spoil' the lift of air over the wings and so help slow the aircraft down or increase the rate of descent. Slats are then extended further, flaps again are pushed out and eventually the landing gear hangs down.

All of these essentials create enormous amounts of drag and change the flying characteristics of the aircraft, making it less maneuverable. In certain conditions, the buildup of ice can add weight and increase drag.

The demand on both the engines and pilots is at its peak. If something goes wrong, or the conditions are inclement, it can cause the workload to increase dramatically in an instant. The reaction time of the aircraft is slower in this configuration, especially the engines which may be running at idle on approach descent.

Below 10,000 feet, a sterile cockpit rule is in force—there must be no non-essential chatter. As we shall see it was a rule, along with many others, that was ignored the night of the Colgan Air Flight 3407 crash, which also revealed a deadly litany of work practices within the airline industry that had put tens of millions of lives at risk for many years.

*

The Bombardier Dash 8 Q400 descended in darkness amid a mixture of wintry weather, its twin Pratt and Whitney turboprop engines throbbing in unison. Captain Marvin Dean Renslow asked his co-pilot Rebecca Shaw to make a radio call to operations in Buffalo, to inform them of their imminent arrival in ten to fifteen minutes.

The forty-seven year-old Captain Renslow lived with his wife, young son and daughter in Lutz, Pasco County, Florida. He had joined Colgan Air in September 2005 and had since flown 3,379 hours with the company, 109 of those hours as Pilot in Command of the Q400 model.

Twenty-four year-old First Officer Rebecca Shaw was working her dream job and that Thursday night was delighted to be sitting with a captain who was jovial, friendly and outgoing. She had accumulated 772 hours flying time on the Bombardier Dash 8. It was late evening; the time 22:07 local.

The Buffalo Approach controller cleared them to descend. Captain Renslow took the radio calls, while Shaw pushed the PA button and made her public address to the passengers and flight attendants.

'Folks, from the flight deck your first officer speaking, uh, it looks like at this time we're about ten maybe fifteen minutes outside of Buffalo. Weather in Buffalo is, uh, pretty foggy. Snowing a little bit there it's not too terribly cold, uh, but, uh, at this time I'd like to make sure everybody remains in their seats so the flight attendants can prepare the cabin for arrival. Thank you.'

Shaw had slept little in the last thirty-six hours, having commuted to work from the West Coast to the East Coast,

spending the night in the busy crew lounge where 'one of the seats had her name on it'.

Listening to her PA announcement were forty-five passengers.

They were under the care of two flight attendants busy preparing the cabin for landing. Flight attendant Matilda Quintero, a widow and breast cancer survivor, lived in Woodbridge New Jersey with her ninety year-old mother and one of her two grown daughters.

Quintero usually worked short flights to avoid long stays away from home and had swapped off a flight to Europe so that she could be home that weekend. However, her preferred duty on the Las Vegas sector which included an overnight was changed to the Buffalo flight at the last minute.

The second flight attendant, Donna Prisco, was a mother of four who'd started flying as a flight attendant a year earlier and loved her new job. The two were an exceptional team and made a distinct impression on all those who worked with or flew with them as passengers.

They were taking care of, among others, Alison Des Forges, a human rights activist and world-renowned expert on Rwanda. She was on her way home from a public debate with a member of the British Parliament.

Also on her way to Buffalo was Beverly Eckert whose husband was killed in the 9/11 attacks. She had met with President Obama the previous week and he called her 'an inspiration.' Among them was off-duty Captain Joseph Zuffoletto, travelling as a passenger.

It was now 22:09 and the pilots were well into the approach. Captain Renslow bantered with Shaw. 'How are the ears?'

'Uh they're stuffy.'

'Are they poppin?'

'Yeah.'

'Okay. That's a good thing.'

'Yeah. I wanta make 'em pop.'

The two of them laughed. Shaw had been feeling under the weather and had considered calling in sick for the flight. 'Is that ice on our windshields?' she asked.

'Got it on my side. You don't have yours?'

'Oh yeah, oh, it's lots of ice,' she replied.

The Bombardier Q400 has sophisticated anti-icing devices on the leading edge of its wings as well as parts of its tail and horizontal stabilizer.[4]

The propeller blades themselves are fitted with an electrical de-icing system. The crew had activated the anti-ice system eleven minutes after takeoff.

Automatic weather information issued by the airport at Buffalo was reporting a blustery night in a visibility of 3 miles in light snow and mist, with the temperature a chilly 1 degree. Not threatening but less than ideal conditions demanding a higher workload of the crew.

The aircraft leveled off at four thousand feet and Shaw once again broached a subject they had explored throughout the flight—how some of her co-pilot colleagues had complained about a slow company progression to captain.

'No, but all these guys are complaining. They're saying, you know, how we were supposed to upgrade by now and they're complaining. I'm thinking you what? I really wouldn't mind going through a winter in the northeast before I have to upgrade to captain.'

'No, no.' Captain Renslow replied.

'I've never seen icing conditions. I've never de-iced. I've never seen any....I've never experienced any of that. I don't want to have to experience that and make those kinds of calls. You know I'd have freaked out. I'd have like, seen this much ice and thought, oh my gosh we were going to crash.' Shaw then answered a radio call from Buffalo Approach who continued to vector them towards the localizer for their approach on runway 23.

At 22:15 Captain Renslow reduced the engine power and called for gear down as they were told to contact Buffalo Tower. 'Colgan thirty four zero seven, contact tower one two zero point five. Have a good night.'

Along with the ice threat, winds buffeted the aircraft but these conditions were not exceptional. Level at 2400 feet now, the autopilot was still engaged and the crew had their approach clearance. The aircraft was on a typical flight path with the flaps set at 5 degrees.

Immersed in murky cloud, the Q400's landing lights illuminated moisture that flashed by either side at 180 knots as they headed towards runway 23. Everything was in place for a normal approach and landing, except for one important detail—the speed was dropping. The Q400 requires 20 knots of airspeed to be added to the approach speed in the event of icing but this standard item had not been done.

A double chime sounded, indicating the landing gear was now down and locked. 'Gear's down,' confirmed Shaw.

The combination of landing gear along with the flatter pitch of the propellers turned the aircraft from less than clean, due to some ice, to 'dirty'.

These items added drag and the speed reduced rapidly, from 170 knots to 149 knots, a slow speed for the flaps set only to five at that point.

Captain Renslow called, 'Flaps fifteen, before landing checklist.'

At this point Shaw paused for three seconds and only put the flaps to ten. Perhaps she noticed the already ominous speed reduction as she began to say, 'Uhhh' before both control columns began to judder—a mechanism fitted in some aircraft and *called* a 'stick-shaker' that warns pilots they are flying at a dangerously slow speed.

The automation reached the point where it could no longer cope and the autopilot-disconnect horn sounded. The horn continued to blare out a warning for the remainder of the flight.

The flaps were still on their way out and were only passing 6.7 degrees as the speed dropped to a dangerously low 126 knots. Then, for reasons that will never be known, Captain Renshaw pulled back on the control column: an act in itself that decreased the speed further as he increased the pitch of the aircraft, up to 30 degrees and so now the wing's angle of attack came even closer to the stalling angle. He did increase the power a little to 70 percent of total torque power; however, the Bombardier Q400 could go to 130 percent of total torque in an emergency, so it had plenty of power remaining to help take it away from a stall situation.

Nevertheless, Captain Renshaw never demanded more than 80 of that 130 percent.

The automatic stick-pusher physically pushed against the control column in an attempt to increase the aircraft's speed.

Captain Renslow overrode it by increasing his backward pull on the stick.

The Airspeed now dropped to 100 knots.

Only seven seconds had passed since the stick shaker indicated an imminent stall.

The aircraft was now pitched up at an angle of 23 degrees. The nose fell and they rolled right to a bank of 110 degrees. Captain Renslow uttered, 'Jesus Christ' and Shaw put the flaps handle back to zero and said, 'I put the flaps up.' She then asked: 'Should the gear be up?'

'Gear up, oh shit.' There was an increase in the ambient noise in the cockpit. In a chilling moment, Captain Renslow realized it was over. 'We're down.'

Rebecca Shaw's microphone relayed to the voice recorder her last words at 22:16 and 51 seconds—only 25 seconds had passed since the first indication of a problem via the aircraft's stick shaker. 'We're—' she said, followed by a scream.

Two seconds later the recording stopped.

The remains of Colgan Air Flight 3407

All forty-five passengers and the four crew died, along with one victim on the ground. Fifty deaths, as we shall see in the following pages, happened needlessly and at root, because of an industry's relentless pursuit of profit.

Glenn Meade/Ray Ronan

Yet because of those preventable deaths a profound examination of aviation law was on the horizon—one that in essence, some would claim, reveals a long-standing and almost criminal disregard for human life within the aviation industry in America, and worldwide, for over six decades.

Chapter 12

The Aftermath of the Colgan Air Crash

Fatigue Doesn't Show Up In Autopsies.

'Our problem is we have made flying too safe and so the temptation for management to take chances is too great for them to resist...'

The Colgan Air crash is now considered a Loss of Control or an LOC accident. It is one of at least ten LOC accidents in the last ten years accounting for close to **one thousand five hundred deaths** over that period.

But can the blame be simply placed one hundred percent on the pilots? And if not, what else contributed to this tragedy?

On May 12th at the National Transportation Safety Board's hearing on Flight 3407, the mindset of Colgan Air was slated and a litany of problems revealed within the company that continue to exist in aviation. The crash evidence would educate the North American public's perception of the aviation industry and how it is managed and administered—and it would reveal much about the industry's pilots, their work habits, and their lot.

In fact, the evidence would shake aviation administrators to the core and invoke changes in US law, changes that would send a momentous wake-up call to aviation worldwide—a wake-up call, we contend, that many outside of the US are still choosing to ignore.

*

The disturbing evidence presented showed that Captain Renslow and his co-pilot Rebecca Shaw were probably flying while suffering from fatigue.

But was fatigue a factor in this crash?

The board revealed both pilots at the controls of flight 3407 lived far from their base of operations in Newark and commuted quite some distance to get there. This did not appear to be of their own choosing, but the low salaries paid, and the fact that the airline was continually closing and opening new bases put the pilots in this position. Barbara Hersman of the National Transportation Safety Board said, 'I think it would be a challenge to expect people, within 60 days, to relocate. Especially if they're getting paid $16,000 a year.'

Mr. Morgan, a representative of Colgan Air disagreed. 'It is what works for the airline to put airplanes in places where they need to be flying and we try to adjust our bases as best we can, but we first and foremost have an airline to run'.

First and foremost don't they have passenger safety to consider?

As the hearing into Flight 3407 progressed it quickly became clear how these two pilots worked in an environment of chronic pilot-fatigue. It's a situation experienced by many pilots worldwide.

"'Passengers Deserve Better," Chesley Sullenberger told ABC News reporter Brian Ross during one of his many in-depth investigative reports into pilot fatigue. The image below is a screen capture from footage shot by a pilot of crash-pads and fellow crew having to use rooms in operations centers to catch up on sleep, notably in La Guardia, New York.

abc news photo of a pilot sleeping in an operations center at La Guardia[5]

First Officer Rebecca Shaw had moved back to Washington State on the west coast to save money by living with her parents. To continue employment with Colgan Air it meant her having to constantly commute across the US continent.

Safety board member Kitty Higgins commented: 'Fatigue has been compared to essentially being drunk.

It has the same effect on an individual as alcohol… when you put together the commuting patterns, the pay levels… I think it's a recipe for an accident and that's what we have here.'

Seconds To Disaster

81

Colgan management insisted fatigue was not a problem at their company.

This remark is often echoed over and over by aviation industry management worldwide. Because changes to work patterns could cost money, and because first and foremost many airlines are profit driven, safety comes second. The NTSB's chairman, Rosenker, said of Colgan Air: 'I am concerned about the winking and nodding that I have seen in some of the policies of the company, your company, and crew members, and I don't believe it is only within your company or those crew members.'

Other damning revelations were made by the NTSB.

The experience level in the cockpit was also questioned. (An issue we will re-examine when we return to the Air France Flight 447 crash later.)

There is an informal rule in commercial aviation known as the 'Two thousand hour rule'. To ensure a balance of experience, the combination of the two pilot's experience in that type of aircraft should amount to at least two thousand hours. This would ensure inexperienced pilots only flew with experienced pilots.

Captain Dean Renslow and his co-pilot Rebecca Shaw had less than a thousand hours on type between them.

Was lack of training for the pilots a factor? Why didn't Captain Renslow have adequate training on the aircraft's stall warning and recovery? (A situation, as we shall see, that was similar to the lack of training experienced by the crew of Air France Flight 447.)

The NTSB asked why the pilots were trained for stalls in the simulator up to the point, but not including, when the automatic stick-pusher actually pushed down on the control column, a situation which meant Captain Renslow was not physically familiar with this procedure of stall recovery.

In response, a Colgan Air manager said he would have to read about it.

Was the FAA complicit? The safety board was concerned as to why problems at Colgan Air were missed in previous audits.

A year before the accident an FAA inspector, Christopher J. Monteleon, highlighted deficiencies after a Colgan Air assessment. He was suspended and given a desk job. [6]

This revelation of the FAA's actions led New York Times aviation analyst Bob Miller to suggest: 'Now it's beginning to look like there's some complicity with the FAA and Colgan Airlines in the operation and training of that aircraft.'[7]

So what has changed?

On October 14th 2011, the US House of Representatives passed a bill forcing the FAA and airlines to boost regional airline safety through enhanced training and hiring requirements and by initiating fatigue countermeasures.

'This bill raises the safety bar for all US airlines,' said Capt. John Prater, president of the Air Line Pilots Association, Int'l (ALPA). 'Now, every airline will have an incentive to hire the best-qualified candidates and provide their pilots with the high-quality training they seek and require to maintain the highest possible standard of safety.'

While the US has begun to lead the way in its recommendations, many of the dangerous practices highlighted still exist in aviation internationally.

As for Colgan Air, its management faced no charges; in fact, they produced a report in which they put the blame one hundred percent on the crew. It has to be asked: was the disaster a damning indictment of a company's reckless disregard for safety, ostensibly in the pursuit of more profit?

Might this mindset doom the aviation industry to yet more tragic disasters? Perhaps, unless a fair and equitable balance is found between cost, passenger and crew safety, and company and shareholder profit.

In the wake of the Colgan Air crash of February 2009, experience levels of new pilots to the US industry were increased from 250 hours of piloting a real airplane, to 1,500 hours, before they could obtain a license to fly with an airline. The quality of their 1500 hours and what level of supervision and development is still open to debate.

In Europe the introduction of a new license allows airlines to have pilots with less than 250 hours flying experience entering the cockpits of commercial airliners. The safety margin is being cut so close that it could even prove fatal.

Despite the world becoming a global village, despite instant communications, many of the lessons learned from accidents and incidences fail to travel well.

Pilot fatigue must be tackled. Is overworked, cheap labor in the cockpit conducive to a safe flight? Long commutes forced on pilots have to be curtailed. Finally, training beyond simple box-ticking must be introduced if the industry wishes to avoid future catastrophes by putting passenger and crew lives at risk.

But until airlines and regulators agree to truly put the passenger first, and the recommendations proposed after the Colgan Air crash are adopted worldwide, many more aviation disasters are only waiting to happen. And many millions of passengers' lives will continue to be put at risk.

Chapter 13

How Technology is Changing Aviation

A Marriage for Better and for Worse

'A hundred years ago, it could take you the better part of a year to get from New York to California; whereas today, because of equipment problems at O'Hare, you can't get there at all.' ~ Dave Barry (Only Travel Guide you'll ever need)

Aircraft are becoming more and more sophisticated and yet this statement will disturb readers; frighteningly, a widely spoken phrase by pilots in response to an aircraft's odd behavior is, 'What is it doing now?'

Meaning that spurious behavior by the aircraft's onboard computers has caused an inadvertent action to be performed by the automation. From computers turning the aircraft in the wrong direction, to every display in front of the pilots suddenly turning blank, glitches do occur. They occur more often than you would think, but pilots generally tend to cope.

US Federal Aviation Administration's chief scientific and technical adviser, Dr Kathy Abbott, does not believe computers are ready to replace pilots, who 'successfully deal with seventy percent of unanticipated failures, let alone the failures for which there was a checklist'.[8]

To reduce the workload on the pilots and enable them to deal with the current aircraft flight situation and to plan ahead, the flying can be done and the systems monitored by computers.

When the first fly-by-wire Airbus was under production, an unofficial phrase coming from the heart of Europe was that the most expensive passenger seat on the aircraft would be that of the pilot. Which may be partly the reason that pilots are being 'designed out' of the aircraft, when in reality, the intelligence of the automation is not yet good enough to do the pilot's job.

The pilots sit at the nose of what can be very large planes, locked away behind a cockpit door and isolated from the flight attendants, and also 'in essence' isolated from the aircraft systems. 'More importantly is the mental isolation caused by the nature of the controls,' says Donald Norman of UC San Diego.

Another problem is that the automation does exactly what it should up to this point, relieving the workload on the pilots but taking them 'out of the loop.' But often when something goes wrong there is no warning or obvious lead up as the automation provides no running commentary on its operations to the flight crew; as was the case, we will see in the next chapter, with the pilots of the Air France Flight 447.

Pilots who one minute were sitting in relative peace can be abruptly plunged into a maelstrom of failures and warnings.

One such example was the explosion of an engine onboard a Qantas Airbus A380 on November 4th 2010. Severe damage to other parts of the aircraft caused fifty seven separate warnings to be generated by the automated systems, which were presented to the pilots in the cockpit.

Faced with such an onslaught of failures, the captain, Richard De Crespigny, decided to identify what systems he and his crew still had operational and how to safeguard and use these systems. This onslaught of failures is in essence what is becoming known in the aviation industry as a 'Black Swan' event: an incident that is entirely unforeseeable. In this case, due to the severe nature of the damage caused when the engine exploded.

Much of the automation was sidelined in this case by the pilots in a successful attempt at simplifying the situation. It was a decision that likely saved the lives of the passengers and crew on board.

The destroyed engine on QF32

On March 1st 2008, Lufthansa flight 44 from Munich to Hamburg attempted to land in strong winds of up to 47 knots. The left main wheel touched down and so the computers switched from 'flight mode' to 'ground mode'. However, the aircraft was not yet firmly placed on the runway, and the crew lost the control they needed due to the computer law changeover designed into the Airbus 320 they were flying. Despite 60 tons of plane and all its momentum, they were now at the mercy of the wind that swept the aircraft towards the runway edge, and as a result the wingtip of the A320 struck the tarmac.

The flying pilot slammed forward the throttles to abort the landing and made a go around; this decision by the pilots saved the day. Within seconds of this action the computers understood the pilots wanted to get airborne once more and so handed back full control.

132 passengers and 5 crew escaped disaster that day. Investigators found the wind limits laid down by the manufacturer and the operator were not only confusing, but there were varying interpretations by pilots and the airlines about what you can actually do with that model of aircraft. Also the control laws created a 'glitch', a moment when the onboard automation didn't recognize the situation.

'No handbook tells you the plane will do this,' a senior Lufthansa pilot told Der Spiegel. [9] Another Black Swan event?

The problem, it appears, is not that the automation is too powerful, but not powerful enough. It is not truly 'aware', according to Donald Norman, and in the human sense cannot self-monitor; therefore it cannot always give the pilots the total feedback they need to alert them to a potential problem.

Such feedback is essential if equipment does fail and unexpected events—Black Swan events—occur.

In the words of David Learmount, of Flight Global: 'There has been a loss of pilot exposure to anything other than pre-packaged flight planning, followed by automated flight.'

He believes the atrophying of their skills must be reversed: 'Airlines must rebuild the pilot skills that automation takes away from them.'

Leaning heavily on automation to save the day, the airline industry strives to shorten the pilot training route, to lengthen flight duty hours and increase work schedules. This is raising a lot of concerns among seasoned professionals; one such result could be a generation of pilots with low experience and a dependency on automation.

'Automation reduced the workload, the pressures in the cockpit and helped reduce accidents. That pressure is reappearing with the arrival of the low fares frenzy. But the carpet is fraying at the edges and is about to unravel,' says a seasoned captain, who has over ten thousand hours with an airline headed towards a new low fares philosophy. He worries that dependency on automation is seeding complacency.

Much of the training and simulator testing done today was intended for older aircraft and hasn't kept pace with high tech design let alone automation.

Crew training has to change to take into account the psychology of pilots on the flight deck. The industry and regulators need to get serious. A complete review of cockpit automation and training for pilots is called for in order to prepare them for when their onboard automation might fail.

Such a review also requires improved communication from the aircraft's automation, so as to aid flight crews recognize quickly the exact nature of what has gone wrong.

Accident chronicles may record human error, but on the many occasions when technically troubled flights are saved by airline crews they are often not made publically known, or even exposed within an airline. The Miracle on the Hudson was one such Black Swan event that did achieve worldwide attention for obvious reasons.

But unfortunately, not all technical disasters are overcome.

Chapter 14

Air France Flight 447

The Aftermath of a tragedy

Many things that are wrong with the airline industry converged on the tragic night over the Atlantic when AF447 disappeared. As always with any accident, it poses many questions, not least of which is why so many passengers and crew lost their lives in a calamitous accident that never should have happened.

According to the French investigators, the catalysts for this tragedy were small but potentially harmful ice crystals that blocked up the aircraft's pitot tubes.

Poking out from the aircraft skin, these pitot tubes measure the inflow of air so that the aircraft's computers may calculate current speed and altitude.

That night over the Atlantic as first officers Robert and Bonin checked their radar due to thunderstorm activity in their vicinity, they discussed icing risks, which was standard procedure for their route of flight.

Meanwhile, tiny ice crystals began to form inside the pitot tubes.

Manufactured by Thales, these tubes had a known history of technical problems due to icing.

As first officers Robert and Bonin flew their aircraft in the vicinity of the thunderstorms, suddenly the autopilot and the automatic thrust of the engines tripped out and the previously tranquil flight deck plummeted into a cascade of alarms. Synthetic voices shouted out warnings and the aircraft speed displayed on the pilot's screens became unreliable and confusing.

The Airbus computers, which would normally prevent the pilots from moving the aircraft into a dangerous flight condition, abruptly handed back control to the crew.

But how could experienced pilots lose control of their aircraft?

The instant transition from a normal flight into a possible life threatening scenario may have plunged the two first officers into an information overload, overwhelming them. In the words of David Learmount of Flight Global, 'the pilots were confronted with a situation they clearly didn't recognize, or didn't believe, or didn't understand.'[1]

Did the cockpit design contribute to the disaster?

(A new human factors sub group created within the AF447 investigation team will likely offer some important conclusions about this question and ought to be noted in the final report.)[2]

The Airbus design is one of the most complex of any aircraft, in that it relies heavily - if not completely - on computers. Airbus design philosophy is such that reliance of onboard computerization is almost taken to the point of infallibility.

In a 1994 documentary called Fatal Logic, German journalist Tim Van Beveren challenged the concept of infallibility assumed by not only airbus designers but by the founder of the fly-by-wire philosophy.

(Fly-by-wire is an automated system of control of the aircraft, which eliminates certain controls which were formally of a mechanical nature.)

Van Beveren interviewed at length the spiritual father of automation in the cockpit, Bernard Ziegler of Airbus.[3] When presented with a significant fault discovered by pilots regarding the A340 aircraft design software, Zeigler admitted that even an aircraft as automated as an Airbus cannot cope with every eventuality. 'This is one of the highly remote probabilities where you really need a crew to interpret. You cannot cover such low probabilities with a computer'.[4]

According to Van Beveren, the airing of this comment was blocked by Airbus but is still available on the documentary.

Airbus aircraft have protections built in which are meant to safeguard it from becoming 'upset'—a term that means an unusual flight angle in which the aircraft may no longer keep flying; such as a stall. For instance, the protections will not allow the pilots to bank the airplane past 67 degrees. In Airbus Terminology this is called 'Normal Law'.

However, in the event of certain computer failures then the aircraft can end up in what is known as 'Alternate Law', and in this law you lose many of the 'Airbus protections'.

In the Air France 447 case it wasn't that the computers failed, they did what they were designed to do: in other words,

when the information is so conflicting that the computer can no longer cope, it hands back control to the pilots.

Three computers calculate speed. With conflicting information from the pitot tubes blocked by ice crystals they simply said: 'we give up', causing a cascade of computer confusion and resignation. This resulted in the change from Normal Law to Alternate Law and among other things the loss of autopilot and the auto thrust.

Seconds To Disaster

95

So did the automation fail? The pilots were handed an aircraft that was in 'Alternate Law', without many of the computer generated protections against 'upset'. However, when Airbus introduced fly-by-wire aircraft they claimed there was no longer the need to train pilots on how to take control in the event of the aircraft becoming unstable, or 'upset', especially at high altitude.

Airbus states in its training manuals, 'the effectiveness of fly-by-wire architecture, and the existence of control laws, eliminates the need for upset recovery manoeuvres to be trained in protected Airbus aircraft.'[5]

But a source inside the French pilots union SNPL (Syndicat National des Pilotes de Ligne) confessed, 'We discussed that item many times with Airbus test pilots and some engineers. They stated the opposite. That if you lost the protections you will *need* to be trained against an upset or worse…'[6]

Experts, investigators and the Air France pilots believe it is exactly this type of training that may have saved the day, and prevented the tragedy of AF447.[7]

The real point is that most pilots just don't get high altitude upset training unless the airline *opts* to do so.

'They never have the chance to practice recovery manoeuvres,' says Chesley Sullenberger, the captain of the Miracle on the Hudson aircraft.

The reality is that Air France pilots were not trained for the catastrophic situation that developed on AF 447— because Airbus said there was no need.

We must remember that the Captain of the Colgan Air Flight 3407 crash, Marvin Renslow, did not have sufficient stall training, or upset recovery training—exactly as was the case with the Air

France pilots.

There was no captain on the flight deck of Air France 447 when things started to go wrong.

The public would be right in asking why.

To fly long-haul obviously requires long flight times and demands long duty days for the pilots and flight attendants. Common to most long-haul companies and on long-haul flights, the law demands that airlines roster an additional pilot.

For the airlines the cheapest option is for that extra pilot to be a first officer and not a captain. This first officer is known as a 'cruise' or 'relief' pilot.

On AF 447, being a long haul flight, there was one captain and two first officers.

The practise may vary among airlines but here's how it works: over a thirteen hour flight say, the aircraft may be in a cruise for twelve hours. Some of this cruise time will be divided into three break periods for the pilots, which could last from three to four hours.

Cockpit voice recordings retrieved from the black box reveal that as the disaster began to develop,

First Officer Robert pushed the call button several times to summon Captain Dubois.

It's not known for sure if the captain was asleep in his bunk, but the rest area is immediately outside of the cockpit and accessed through a secure door.

It took a minute and a half for Captain Dubois to return; an eternity in aviation terms when, in the midst of an emergency, seconds can count. (Some airlines using Airbus aircraft actually removed the pilot rest area outside the cockpit so that extra business class seating could be fitted. In this instance pilots have to use the flight attendant's rest area, located halfway down the aircraft. This increases the amount of time it would take for a pilot to return to the cockpit in an emergency situation.)

Another problem compounded the unfolding crisis.

The Airbus' electronic flight instrument systems are constructed in such a way that if all the primary systems fail—in other words, if there is a major loss of instruments—the standby instruments that are used as back-up are located close to the **captain's** seated position. In the event of a loss of electrical generation, the emergency electrical power will supply **only** the captain's instrument panel.

So now the **least** experienced pilot onboard the aircraft found himself in a situation where he was hand-flying on only the most basic instrumentation and in a possible disaster scenario. In this case, it involved flying through a dangerous thunderstorm with no external radar to help navigate the storm cells.

The two first officers on board AF447 were respected and skilful, but they desperately needed the experience of their captain when things started to unravel.

Unfortunately, it appears there was no time for Captain Dubois to get back to the cockpit and grasp a full understanding of the emergency before the aircraft crashed. Some long-haul captains freely admit that they hardly manage to sleep well during their assigned break; they toss and turn, getting no rest.

Perhaps having another captain on the flight deck would ease their anxiety, and allow them to benefit from the rest they are required to take under aviation law.

But it remains to be seen whether airlines are prepared to incur

Glenn Meade/Ray Ronan

that extra cost to safeguard passengers' lives.

Incidences similar to Air France 447's pitot failures have occurred in the past with airlines using the same Thales manufactured pitot tubes.

Some of those failures led to loss of speed indications at high altitudes due to icing during cruise—again similar to Air France 447. These failures prompted many exchanges between Airbus and Air France to determine whether or not to replace the Thales pitot tubes with a new model, by the same manufacturer. Airbus asked Air France to wait for better models to become available by Thales, but stated that a more recent Thales model performed better in icing. Air France ordered and had just received a shipment of these replacements in the week leading up to the disaster.

A complicating factor for the pilots is that Airbus announced that erroneous stall warnings could sound in the event of a pitot blockage—information that conflicts with standard procedures dictating that all stall warnings should always be respected.

Since the AF447 disaster, all Air France aircraft are now equipped with American Goodrich pitot tubes, not Thales.

This poses a vital question: was there a failure on behalf of the regulators to push Airbus and Thales for quicker replacement of the pitot tubes?

The fact is that this type of phenomenon occurred in many other airlines, although not exactly in the same conditions.

A selection of 13 cases of similar pitot tube failure was cited by the French Air Accident investigators, BEA, which looked into the AF 447 crash:[8]

Air France (4 cases)

TAM (2 cases)

Qatar Airways (4 cases)

Northwest (1 case)

Air Caraïbes Atlantique (2 cases)

The BEA interviewed pilots from these flights. 'The crews did not understand what had happened at the time and NONE of them called for the appropriate checklist or carried out the memorized response....due to the surprise and lack of training.'

Surprise, lack of training, the lack of a commander in the flight deck, lack of timely replacement of faulty pitot tubes, and the unwillingness to upgrade the aircraft with a computerised angle of attack system that could have prevented the Air France crash— what all of these contributing factors are about is cost.

In the end, passengers died needlessly because of cost.

As tragic as Air France 447 was, this disaster will be analysed for decades to come and we hope that the loss of passenger and crew lives will not be in vain. And that in their memory the industry will strive toward ever safer skies for everyone.

Chapter 15

The Future of Flying

What Can be Done to Make Things Better?

'You never know on which flight your career will be judged.' - *NTSB*

Veteran aviation employees will tell you that airline people used to run airlines and they knew the business—they loved the idea of flight, loved the industry and understood that it was unique. Harnessing nature and carrying humans aloft to where they wish to go is not foolproof, but it has great rewards. However, it demands incredible foresight and preparedness.

Unscrupulous elements see this skill and a love for the industry as a weakness. They exploit it, while stealing each day another small piece from the safety envelope, viewing pilots and others as— 'lemons, I squeeze until they are dry'— this comment from a major low fares airline CEO about his pilots.

Your safety is—among others—in the hands of those pilots who fly you, the flight attendants who evacuate you, the engineers who service those planes and the air traffic controllers who help guide the increasing amount of air traffic.

Their caliber, the quality of their training and their mental and physical health must be a priority.

But what if the pursuit of profit interferes with a safe company? An airline may have a string of major safety issues without the flying public ever knowing; even the crews flying with that airline may be kept in the dark.

As we've seen, because many reports are withheld either by those involved, by airlines or regulators, the true number of incidences is unknown.

Mary Schiavo, former Inspector General of the United States Department of Transportation, suggests airlines that continually fail to adhere to the rules, and generate high numbers of safety violations, should be fined, publically and a list disseminated to the travelling public. Chesley Sullenberger believes there should be a worldwide safety web, where safety issues can be shared. 'How much safer we would be if we had this system,' an investigator working on the AF447 disaster told us. But to do that regulators themselves need more funding— not less, as is often the trend—if they are to be independent from and uninfluenced by the industry they govern.

We've discussed much throughout our journey in this book and hope it will generate debate, and hopefully some action. Aviation is considered safe because it has always been predicated on an improving rate of reducing fatal accidents. The worrying trends we highlight in this book have halted that improvement and risk reversing it if regulators in particular don't listen to the concerns of those on the frontline.

Regular flyers should perhaps take a moment to send one email, reminding regulators of their obligation to **you**, the passenger, not to the airlines.

Don't doubt that your mail will make a difference; look at recent events where social media has changed nations. Contact any public representative, tell them to step up to the plate and do their job.

As for what else you can do, put more consideration into what kind of airline you want to fly with in future. In many ways how an airline treats its passengers may be a reflection of how that same airline treats its employees. And from this you may well assume the condition of their safety culture.

To some degree, your safety is also in your own hands. Make wise and informed decisions on the basis of the information in this book and you, your family and loved ones ought to remain safe when flying.

Chapter 16

Top Tips for Flying Safe

What you can do before and after you buy a ticket to make your flight a safer one:

1. Avoid airlines **banned** by the European Union.

2. Avoid airlines from FAA **downgraded** countries.

3. Avoid carriers under industrial strife; they may hire-in temporary crews or other carriers to help maintain the flight schedule.

4. Low cost does not at once mean low safety; but as the industry fights to survive, it can.

5. Although you book with a major airline, the chances are growing in Europe, as it may be in the US, that a smaller carrier was contracted to do the flight. Some are good, some are bad. Ask which regional carrier you'll be flying with, and do yourself a favor and check their safety record online before you fly.

6. If flying with children, use a proper safety harness as described in this book, and not a loop belt.

7. When and where possible, avoid flying in extremes of weather, and especially with smaller carriers.

8. When possible, avoid flying in world regions where air accidents are more common and air safety does not always appear to be paramount: most of Africa, parts of the Russian Federation.

If you have to, then do not fly with airlines mentioned in tip 1, 2 and 3.

9. Prefer a seat in the 'survival' zone.

The Survival Zone in an aircraft—what is it?

According to studies, some seats offer a higher percentage of survivability in certain accidents where an evacuation is required.

The world leading Fire Safety Group at Greenwich University led by Professor Ed Galea, studied more than a hundred plane crashes and interviewed almost two thousand survivors.

They found an interesting statistic: the majority of survivors in fatal accidents had only to move 5 seat rows or less to an exit. Less surprising perhaps, those in an aisle seat had a slightly higher survival percentage rate than those seated in window seats.

Onboard Aviation Safety Tips

A comment that crews often hear from their non-aviation friends is: 'The safety demonstration—big deal I've seen it before and anyway if we crash we are dead.'

Wrong.

Over ninety-five percent of passengers in accidents survive but many of the five percent died because of incorrect actions before, during and after the accident. And no matter how often you travel, most people's motor actions are not trained for such an event. In a crash or major incident you may have to rely on tired and overworked flight attendants to show you the way out of a life threatening situation, so educate yourself.

Here's an abbreviation which some airlines use to instill instinctive reactions in their crews: **S.O.S.** = **S**urvive the impact, get **O**utside, **S**urvive outside.

S.O.S.

Survive the impact.

That announcement onboard asking you to pay attention even if you are a regular traveler; they aren't kidding. Just like the pilots and flight attendants, practice does make perfect and where survival is concerned, appropriate reactions are worth striving for.

Imagine if someone hit you with a baseball bat then held your head over a barbeque -that's how it may feel in the case of an accident. You'd be hard pushed to think clearly about what you should do to get out of the situation. Having survival actions engraved on your brain is the key. History shows even experienced crew get it wrong; if you assume you know what to do because you have seen it before and often, you may want to think twice and put down that newspaper.

Here's an example: you travel by car much more often than you fly. Picture yourself trying to get out of that car in a hurry for any reason you want. What is the first thing you'll do? You'll push down on the seatbelt release to free yourself from restraint. In the event of an aircraft accident or incident you may in all probability push down on that seatbelt release because it's what you are used to doing, and it won't work. According to Professor Ed Galea, this is a common occurrence in accidents and has led to deaths.

This universal action is called reversion.

People revert to normal behavior, to predominant actions. Pilots who used to fly one type of aircraft for many years and now fly another are known to revert to procedures for their previous aircraft under stress or fatigue.

Flight attendants flying everyday on different aircraft types open doors without disarming the emergency escape chutes all the time; they assume they know which aircraft they are on and they've seen it before. But they can still get it wrong when they stand at that door and lift instead of lowering, push instead of pull, or arm instead of disarming.

Back to our emergency where you may spend ten seconds or more trying to figure out what you are doing wrong; time in which you should have been trying to escape, and in aircraft accidents, time may not be on your side.

Regulators give manufacturers 90 seconds to empty an aircraft during trials. And in those trials half the exits will fail. However, you can bet that every one of those test passengers were told moments before by their crew to LIFT on the latch to open that belt, and were reminded also of the location of the exits.

Why does this reversion happen even to people who fly many times a week? A certain area of the nervous system takes over in emergencies, preparing you for 'fight or flight', and you go into safemode, or basic mode. If car travel is your predominant method of transport, your brain will revert to this familiar situation. Do yourself a favor and remind the brain before takeoff where you are.

The items displayed in a safety demonstration are carefully selected.

They are your survival tools.

The pilots, the flight attendants, Air Traffic and Emergency Services on the ground, all know what part they will play in the event of something going wrong. The safety demonstration is when you are told your part. It only works if the team is cohesive and you may well find yourself part of that team. Flight attendants may become incapacitated in some way and you could find yourself having to open a door, or if you sit at an overwing exit, you will have to open it in the event of an evacuation.

Oxygen masks may drop down. Put them on at once. Don't ask questions or wait to be told. You may only have seconds before passing out. No matter how silly you feel, or even if you sense nothing wrong, put on the mask—the cockpit crew or the aircraft has obviously detected a problem if the oxygen masks are deployed. It could be a slow leak of pressure with the air in the cabin dwindling away without any apparent indication while you become increasingly happy due to oxygen starvation. You may see the flight attendants grabbing the nearest masks and jumping on a nearby passenger's lap. Meanwhile the pilots could be coping with their full face masks and the inherent restrictions to clear thought and communications they pose. In this case, there may not be an announcement for some time that something may be wrong.

On many aircraft, oxygen masks will drop down automatically above a certain loss of cabin pressure, then an automatic public address will play over and over telling you to sit down - anywhere - put on the mask and strap in. Unless you are in a toilet on a US registered aircraft, where oxygen masks were removed due to security 'concerns', concerns that apparently overrode the safety worries of many who objected. And if your child is travelling on your lap there may only be one mask per seat leaving you with a choice; and remember too that the mask is not really designed with children in mind, so make it a snug fit.

Don't expect to feel a rush of oxygen coming at you from the mask. A chemical process in the system above your head is gently oozing out oxygen at a steady rate for the next fifteen minutes or so, as the aircraft descends to a safe level where the masks are no longer required by passengers and crew. As the demo says, do put on your own mask first, because if you fiddle around with your child's, or your partner's you may well pass out first and not finish the job for either of you.

The brace position. Different airlines may show you slightly different brace positions but they all have the same basic goal; to get you down as low as you can to prevent a whiplash, or 'jackknife' effect on your body. It's getting harder to actually brace yourself with seats crammed ever closer together, but pushing your body forward and down as much as possible will make all the difference. Crash victims who do not adopt this position 'flail' upon impact and fracture limbs and skulls on the seat in front of them.

Rear facing seats, as the military have adopted for decades in its air transports, as well as many business jets, would dramatically improve safety, but public comfort and perceptions prevent it, for now. Business class configurations have used a head to toe seating for some time now. One seat faces forward, with the seat beside facing rearwards. It makes for an airy cabin and there are few complaints about flying backwards. The idea of putting seats head to toe on more flights is being considered because airlines can fit more passengers in that way.

S.O.S.

Get Outside

'It's often claimed that frequent flyers have a good knowledge of the aircraft, and that recent fliers also have a good knowledge of the aircraft layout. Of great concern is the result that only a little more than a quarter of the 'recent frequent flyers' could identify the number of exits, locate their position and identify their relative size,' says Professor Galea, whose group also completed a three and a half year vital study into the 911 evacuation of the twin towers.

A worrying revelation occurred when Galea surveyed aircraft passengers and their exit knowledge. The team discovered that only about twenty-five percent of people knew where the exits were and how small the overwing exits may be.

But does size really matter? In this case it does. The most common aircraft types are narrow body Airbus A320's and Boeing 737's.

During the safety briefing on these aircraft, crew will tell you there are, 'Two at the back, two at the front and two in the middle.' There's a famous phrase plugged by flight attendants, 'there may be more than 50 ways to leave your lover, but only four ways to leave this airplane.'

You should also know that a fire can become uncontrollable on an aircraft in less than two minutes; one of the reasons evacuation certification for an aircraft is 90 seconds, even for the 900 seat Airbus A380.

Glenn Meade/Ray Ronan

Here's the gotcha on smaller aircraft—at those big doors you can walk out; at the smaller overwings, you have to climb out.

Exit size does matter. In many accidents, passengers were crammed at the overwing exits trying to get out, while in front of and behind them the large door exits were moving fast or vacant altogether. In videos of aircraft evacuations, two or three passengers at overwing exits can be seen getting jammed together. 'This inherent lack of exit knowledge is likely to have a negative impact on overall evacuation efficiency and hence passenger safety,' says Galea's group. 'The pre-flight briefing makes no mention of the size of the exits and the impact this may have on evacuation times.' They recommend that passenger briefings emphasize the location and type of exits because irrespective of flight experience, two fifths of passengers surveyed elected to use the smaller, slower overwing exits.

Ed Galea and his team have also found that in **one-third** of accidents analyzed, more than **half** of aircraft exits were unusable due mainly to failure of the door or slide during emergencies. That exit you have your eye on may not be usable. As a passenger, it would be wise to have two exits in mind, not just one. Educate yourself. Remember, not all aircraft doors are created equal, so next time you fly take a moment to see where those exits are, and if you are involved in an evacuation, watch for movement and make your choice wisely.

Remember, it doesn't matter if you fly every day, you are in a non-normal and highly dynamic environment.

Remind your brain where it is.

Keep in mind the five seat row rule.

Keep your shoes on for takeoff and landing: easier to run over burning materiel and for getting away from an aircraft on the ground.

Remember the critical eleven minutes, three minutes after takeoff, eight before landing. Pay attention; be alert. Don't wear headphones, or eye covers during this time.

A common belief is that total panic will ensue in the event of an emergency. Not so. Survivor reports from crew and passengers tell of terrified passengers carrying out instructions and lining up for exits. Crying and shouts can be heard, raised voices, all normal for people with an elevated level of stress.

Pulling out luggage to take with you down that slide may kill not just you but others. This is the main obstruction to aircraft evacuations.

If it isn't in your pocket, leave it behind.

All over the world pilots and flight attendants are amazed as they watch videos of passengers evacuating burning aircraft whilst clutching suitcases and bags, possibly obstructing evacuation, such as the A340 aircraft that overran the runway in Toronto in 2005. 'Although all passengers managed to evacuate, the evacuation was impeded because nearly 50 per cent of the passengers retrieved carry-on baggage,' said Canadian Investigators.

S.O.**S.**

Survive outside.

You've survived the impact, you've got out, now you want to survive outside.

Glenn Meade/Ray Ronan

There's a photograph in circulation of a passenger sitting in a life raft, with an inflated **life vest** wrapped about his neck. He's lucky. If he'd entered the water that way the life vest could either have come off or strangled him.

Watch how to put the vest on correctly; they aren't all the same design.

Even if you are taking off in the midland state of Kansas, you may need a flotation device of some sort. (A wide river wraps about Kansas City Airport, the Missouri.)

Many airports are situated close to or adjacent to water either in the form of a lake, river or the sea, because this offers among other things better take off performance for aircraft—less things to hit on the way out or in: as is the case Chicago, New York JFK, San Francisco, Kansas City, and many more cities.

You don't have to ditch in the sea to require a flotation device or life vest; as runway excursions or runoffs remain one of the main aircraft accidents, aircraft do end up in the water.

Even small commercial aircraft or business jets are taller than you, and if the aircraft is just sitting in water, you may need to get away from it and the surrounding water could be deep, or very fast moving, littered with jagged debris, or coated with aircraft fuel in which it is impossible to swim. You will need to float.

Do Not inflate your life vest before leaving the aircraft, not until you get out. If your aircraft does not have life vests, as on some US internal flights, take a flotation device with you— meaning the seat cushion you have your backside on.

An inflated life jacket will slow you down inside the cabin and will delay you or even prevent you and others from getting out. Most importantly, if water enters the aircraft- as with the Ethiopian Airlines Flight 961 that broke up as it ditched close to the shore - an inflated jacket will cause you to float to the top of the cabin and absolutely prevent any movement or escape. The bodies of many passengers on the Ethiopian aircraft who had survived the initial impact were found inside the cabin with their lifejackets inflated. If you are on an aircraft that does carry lifejackets, have a look to see if your lifejacket is actually there, as they do get stolen. Some cost saving airlines do not carry spares, or carry very few.

ENDS

For further information, source material, updates and links see
secondstodisaster.com/
www.facebook.com/seconds2disaster

AUTHOR BIOGRAPHY

Glenn Meade is a journalist and specialist in the field of commercial flight simulation.

He is the author of nine books, many of them international bestsellers, published in 26 languages, and have earned him critical acclaim. Meade worked in aviation for twenty years.

Ray Ronan is an Airbus A320 Captain and Journalist. He has contributed to aviation safety forums and has instructed during crew training.

Other Books by the Authors:

Glenn Meade

Snow Wolf

Brandenburg

The Sands of Sakkara

Resurrection Day

Web of Deceit

The Devil's Disciple

The Second Messiah

The Romanov Conspiracy

WWW.GlennMeadeAuthor.com

Ray Ronan

Lethal Harvest

USEFUL RESOURCES

Which Airlines are banned from European airspace.
http://ec.europa.eu/transport/air-ban/list_en.htm

Here is the FAA list of downgraded countries. You will need Excel to read this.
http://www.faa.gov/about/initiatives/iasa/

To find out more about Toxic cabin, or what to do if you believe you may have been exposed: **Aerotoxic.org**

Aviation Safety Network "Providing everyone with a (professional) interest in aviation with up-to-date, complete and reliable authoritative information on airliner accidents and safety issues".

Up to date listings of incidents and accidents, not comprehensive.
The Aviation Herald

For child safety onboard aircraft.
kidsflysafe.com

Glenn Meade/Ray Ronan

Child Safety Tips

Fly with an airline that clearly allows an approved car seat. Jan Brown - "Parents should only purchase a car seat that has an FAA or airplane approved sticker."

Information about an airline's safety standard for children can be hard to find, and even crew awareness of their own company's rules may be lax, so print them up and take them with you.

Remember that when flying to Europe from the US, if the company is European they will insist you use the loopbelt. With American companies or aircraft simply registered in the US, then the FAA rules apply.

You will have to purchase a ticket for all children over 2 years anyway so think about a child restraint system certified for use on aircraft such as the 'CARES' system. A belt and buckle device for kids 22-44 pounds, or 10-20 kg, one that is easy to use and creates a safe airplane seat for your child without the hassle of carrying a car seat.[1]

Do not imagine that the airline's safety card will give you all the information you need to know regarding your child's safety, and simply because it shows an adult bracing with a child in its grip means this is safe.

Jan Brown - "When I was still a working flight attendant, one of my flying partners and I read the manual with two differing interpretations....and have had to instruct a parent that the loopbelt was not allowed.

The only positive aspect of the loopbelt remains the fact that they won't missile through the cabin but that seems to be more for passenger protection than for the toddler/infant. There are some airplane safety cards that do not demonstrate an infant at all when showing the emergency brace position while those that do show the parent holding the child with one arm and bracing against the forward seatback with the other arm....now both are in a dangerous position as the parent is in a position to be hit with the overhead contents (as occurred on our Sioux City crash) and if an adult cannot hold a child with TWO arms, it is ludicrous to show a one arm-hold (I brought a 757 and an Airbus safety card to an FAA meeting 2 years ago and nothing has changed!) This indicates that children under two are not given the slightest thought and also leaves flight attendants unable to provide safety for ALL of their passengers...only those over two years of age. Yet flight attendants may be fined by the FAA if they do not instruct passengers to be seated/belted when the seat belt sign is illuminated."

For further information, Jet with Kids is a great resource for parents intending to fly.

REFERENCES:

_____

Chapter 1

[1]http://www.telegraph.co.uk/news/worldnews/southamerica/brazil/5481
061/Air-France-crash-Familys-fear-of-flying-together-led-mother-and-
son-to-board-doomed-Flight-447.html

[2] https://en.wikipedia.org/wiki/ACARS

Chapter 2

[1] http://asrs.arc.nasa.gov/overview/confidentiality.html

[2]ASRS: The Case for Confidential Incident Reporting Systems. PDF.

[3]http://www.easa.europa.eu/communications/press-
releases/2012/EASA-press-release-06012012.html

Chapter 3

[1]Professor Andrew Steptoe and Sophie Bostock of University College
London: A survey of fatigue and well-being among commercial airline
pilots.

[2] http://edition.cnn.com/2012/03/28/travel/airline-crew-mental-health/

Chapter 4

[1] http://jtsb.mlit.go.jp/jtsb/aircraft/download/bunkatsu.html#7

[2] PB2002-910401. NTSB/AAB-02/01. DCA00MA006

[3] US ALPA White Paper: Producing a Professional Airline Pilot.

Chapter 6

[4] http://ec.europa.eu/transport/air-ban/list_en.htm

[5]http://www.flightglobal.com/news/articles/comment-virtual-
airlines-look-real-but-the-security-of-the-product-is-very-different-
353366/

121

[6]http://www.eurocockpit.be/stories/20120306/low-cost-outsourcing-a-new-trend-with-doubtful-benefits-2

[7] The safety culture survey conducted by Illumia of Illinois University is industry recognized, developed by research grants from both the FAA and the US Air Force. Over 190 organizations and airlines have completed the survey. Only one management have refused to take part: US Airways, who in fact refused to sign the non-disclosure agreement, denouncing this revealing safety mechanism as union propaganda.

[8]The safety culture survey by Illumia of Illinois University.

[9]Safety at EasyJet Our Concerns. Safety Day 2011. EPG

[10] Page 2. Q3B sent to EasyJet.

[11] A survey of fatigue and well-being among commercial airline pilots. Final report 7th February 2011.

[12] Professor Andrew Steptoe and Sophie Bostock of University College London: A survey of fatigue and well-being among commercial airline pilots.

[13] NTSB Public Hearing in the matter of: COLGAN AIR, INC. FLIGHT 3407, BOMBARDIER DHC8-400, N200WQ Docket No.: DCA-09-MA-027 CLARENCE CENTER, NEW YORK, FEBRUARY 12, 2009

[14] REPORT ON ACCIDENT TO AIR INDIA EXPRESS BOEING 737-800 AIRCRAFT VT-AXV ON 22nd MAY 2010 AT MANGALORE

[15]http://abcnews.go.com/Blotter/faa-enacts-rules-fight-pilot-fatigue/story?id=15204948#.TygUpPmOefN

[16] Safety at EasyJet Our Concerns. Safety Day 2011. EPG

Chapter 7

[1]http://www.chron.com/news/nation-world/article/Bogus-parts-turn-up-more-often-in-NASA-s-supply-1743967.php

[2] http://defensetech.org/2011/11/08/counterfeit-parts-found-on-new-p-8-posiedons/

[3] AAR96-03

[4] http://www.manilastandardtoday.com/insideMetro.htm?f=2010/july/7/metro2.isx&d=2010/july/7

[5] factor200543

[1] Statement of Jan Brown United 232 Flight Attendant/Survivor, Retired For the Association of Flight Attendants at the NTSB Advocacy Briefing on Child Restraints on Aircraft Washington, DC February 26, 2004

[2] http://www.faa.gov/passengers/fly_safe/turbulence/

[3] Study on Child Restraint Systems Final Report EASA 2007.C.28

[4] Final Report EASA 2007.C.28 'The upper torso and the lower extremities of the infant as well as of the adult sitting behind it break over. The infant moves forward due to its mass inertia forces. The jack-knife movement of the adult triggers so-called wedge expulsion forces which thrust the infant forward even more with the loop belt driving far into the infant's abdomen until it gets hold at the vertebral spine. The adult's head hits against the back of the infant's head, and the adult's chest hits against the infant's back. Due to the high compressive load effective on the child, the adult's legs open and the infant hits onto the ground like a Ping-Pong ball.'

[5] http://www.kidsflysafe.com/

6

http://www.timvanbeveren.de/ENGLISH/welcome aboard.html

[7] Crash Test conducted with TUV-Rheinland, Swiss TV and ARD German Television. Helmond, NL under supervision of Dipl. Ing Martin Sperber, TUV Rheinland.

[8] http://www.faa.gov/passengers/fly_children/crs/

[9] FEDERAL AVIATION ADMINISTRATION RECORDED RADIO PUBLIC SERVICE ANNOUNCEMENT FOR USE ANYTIME, No:60 CHILD SAFETY/"LOVING ARMS"

[10] The National Transportation Safety Board (NTSB) is an independent federal agency charged with determining the probable cause of transportation accidents, promoting transportation safety, and assisting victims of transportation accidents and their families.

[11] NTSB PUBLIC FORUM: CHILD PASSENGER SAFETY IN THE AIR AND IN AUTOMOBILES transcript_12-9-10

[12] http://www.aerospace-technology.com/features/feature48143/

[13] http://www.virgin-atlantic.com/eu/en/travel-information/flying-with-children/children.html

[14] Flying Blind, Flying Safe. Mary Schiavo.

Chapter 9

[15] Boeing 787 Technical Explanation of Change of Air Supply,

Denola-TCP 2011,

MURAWSKI_2011_27(2),

Exposure to tri-o-cresyl phosphate in jet airplane passengers, Mariya Lihasova, Bin Li, Lawrence M. Schopfer, Florian Nachon, Patrick Masson, Clement E. Furlong, Oksana Lockridge.

[16] http://www.dft.gov.uk/publications/cabin-air-quality-faqs/

[17] ACPA_fume_events_newsletter11.01.12_2

[18] The scientific adequacy of the present state of knowledge concerning neurotoxins in

aircraft cabin air. Jeremy J. Ramsden. Cranfield University, Bedfordshire, MK43 0AL, UK

[19] In interview with Tim Van Beveren WDR 2010 'Poison in aircraft'

[20] EASA European Aviation Safety Agency

[21]   http://www.flightglobal.com/blogs/learmount/2011/10/the-bad-smell-that-wont-go-awa.html

Chapter10

[1]http://www.washingtonpost.com/wp-dyn/content/article/2006/04/16/AR2006041600803.html

[2]http://www.aljazeera.com/programmes/peopleandpower/2010/12/2010 1214104637901849.html

[3] Boeing_Internal_report_-_August_21,_2000

Boeing__737__repair_manual

DCIS_MATERIAL_-_PT_1

DCIS_MATERIAL_-_PT_2

DCIS_MATERIAL_-_PT_3

Supp_Report

Case 6:05-cv-01073-WEB Document 70-1 Filed 03/14/2006 TAYLOR SMITH, JEANNINE PREWITT, and JAMES AILES, Plaintiffs and Relators, vs Civil Action No. 05-1073-WEB THE BOEING COMPANY and DUCOMMUN, INC. f/k/a AHF-Ducommun, Defendants.

FAA's Special Technical Audit of Boeing and the Audit Resolution Plan

Chapter 12

[4] The small wings on the tail.

Chapter 13

[5]   http://abcnews.go.com/Blotter/slideshow/inside-secret-world-tired-pilots-12868682

[6]http://www.wivb.com/dpp/news/faa_inspector_saw_problems_with_pl ane_090603

[7]http://www.wivb.com/dpp/news/faa_inspector_saw_problems_with_pl
ane_090603

Chapter 14

[8] http://aerosociety.com/About-Us/bcommittees/lsb

[9] http://www.thelocal.de/national/20090725-20827.html

Chapter 15

[1] http://www.flightglobal.com/blogs/learmount/2011/08/af447-and-the-
loss-of-control.html

[2]http://www.bea.aero/en/enquetes/flight.af.447/info07september2011.e
n.php

[3] Former vice president of engineering, Bernard Ziegler

[4] Fatal Logic, WDR 1995

[5] Airbus A330/A340 Flight Crew Training Manual 01.020 JUL 19/05

[6] omitted.

[7] f-cp090601e3.en_2 4.1 Recommendations on Operations
Bureau d'Enquêtes et d'Analyses pour la sécurité de l'aviation civile
Interim Report n°3 AF447

[8] (1.16 Tests and Research
1.16.3 Study of losses of or temporary anomalies in indicated speeds
occurring in cruise on Airbus A330 / A340

Child Safety:

[1] http://www.kidsflysafe.com/

Made in the USA
San Bernardino, CA
11 January 2015